SECRET INDIANAPOLIS

A GUIDE TO THE WEIRD, WONDERFUL, AND OBSCURE

Have fun exploring!

Ashley Petry

Ashley P

Reedy Press
PO Box 5131
St. Louis, MO 63139
www.reedypress.com

Library of Congress Control Number: 2019940039
ISBN: 9781681062402

Design by Jill Halpin
Unless otherwise indicated, all photos are courtesy of the author or in the public domain. Photo page viii courtesy of Pixabay, photo page 103 courtesy of Downtown Indy, Inc., photo page 94 courtesy of Tiff Whitaker.

Printed in the United States of America
19 20 21 22 23   5 4 3 2 1

CONTENTS

vii .... Acknowledgments
1 .... Introduction
2 .... A Park That's for the Birds
4 .... A Head for Music
6 .... A Fitting Tribute to Fire-Fighting
8 .... A Diner with a Dark (Chocolate) Secret
10 .... A Run of Bad Luck
12 .... A Time-Honored Tradition
14 .... A Breath of Fresh Air
16 .... The Lingerie Legacy
18 .... A Fashionable Address
20 .... An Evening on the Ice
22 .... Indiana's Weirdest Roadside Attraction
24 .... The Whaling Wall
26 .... The House of Blue Lights
28 .... A Curious Costume Contest
30 .... A Museum That Takes Liberties
32 .... A Chamber of Secrets
34 .... An Oasis of Comfort Food
36 .... A Gallery of Graffiti
38 .... A Park with a Purpose
40 .... A Night at the Movies
42 .... The Supreme Sacrifice
44 .... Cultural Imperialism
46 .... Twisted Tresses
48 .... A Friendly Retreat
50 .... A Profile in Courage
52 .... The Boatload of Knowledge

54 ....Food for Thought
56 ....Our Big Fat Greek Frieze
58 .... The Titans of Industry
60 .... The Long Arm of the Law
62 ....A Relic of Dinosaur Digestion
64 ....The Evidence in the Earthworks
66 ....An Office Fit for a Pharaoh
68 ....The Winds of War
70 .... A Statue That Shows a Little Leg
72 ....A Passage to India
74 .... A "Count the Counties" Scavenger Hunt
76 .... An Adventure in Wonderland
78 ....A Tragedy on the Underground Railroad
80 ....The Dream Machine
82 ....An Art Deco Delight
84 ....A Storied Tradition
86 .... A Skyscraper of Ice
106 .... A Presidential Prank
108 ....The Joke of the Week
110 ....An Egg-cellent Way to Travel
112 ....The Power of Love
114 .... A Tutu or Two
116 .... The Great Squirrel Invasion of 1822
118 ....A Real Hatchet Job
120 .... A Pathological History
122 ....The Big Dig
124 .... The Downfall of a Bully
126 ....The Old Order
128 .... A Magnetic Mystery
130 ....A Whirlwind Visit

132 ....The Right Kind of Ramen
134 ....The Art of Deception
136 ....A Room with a View
138 ....The Urban Buzz
140 ....An Officer and a Gentleman
142 ....The Oddness of Otterness
144 ....The Herald of Spring
146 ....The Industrial Arts
148 ....A Tour with a Twist(er)
150 ....Another Boatload of Knowledge
152 ....The City's Largest Costume Party
154 ....The Speedway's Secret Legacy
156 ....A Short Trip Around the World
158 ....A Place to Stew
160 ....An Engine for Change
162 ....Quack in the Pulpit
164 ....A Brutal Architectural Legacy
166 ....The Hoosier Poet
168 ....Oddball Athletics
170 ....History, Repeating Itself
172 ....A Roman Holliday
174 ....An Ocean of Information
176 ....A Home for Gnomes
178 ....A Bitter Theatrical Rivalry
180 ....A Truly Monstrous Mansion
182 ....The Best in Class
184 ....A Shot at Victory
186 ....The Beat of a Different Drummer
188 ....The King of Indy Brews
190 ....The Literary Arts

192 ....A Quick Jaunt to Jamaica
194 .... An Odd Artwork at the Alexander
196 ....The Midnight Train to Nowhere
198 ....An Artsy Way to Stop Traffic
200 .... Sources
209 .... Index

ACKNOWLEDGMENTS

Researching this book has introduced me to the invaluable resources and expertise of organizations such as the Indiana Historical Society, Indiana Landmarks, and Historic Indianapolis. To these organizations: thank you for your incredible efforts to preserve and share the Indianapolis story. I could not have done this without you.

Thanks also to the team at Reedy Press for the support it has provided on this journey, and to my friends and family for the same reason. Especially to Laura, who dropped everything to find me the perfect llama photos. To Sarah, the best saleswoman I know. To Mom, for the delivery of Thanksgiving in a box (even though it was February). And to Will and Cara, my two favorite children on this planet.

The final thank you, as always, is for Michael and Henry. Everything I create in this world is built on the foundation of your love and support, and my bounty is as boundless as the sea.

INTRODUCTION

In many ways my first book wrote itself. Titled *100 Things to Do in Indianapolis Before You Die*, it naturally included the Indy 500, the city's best restaurants and museums, and other popular destinations. Many of the wonderful things about Indy—the weird things, the obscure things—simply didn't make the cut. Here, though, I'm finally able to tell those stories.

This book profiles the city's best-kept restaurant secrets, strangest parks, and weirdest works of art. Also on the list: museums with unusual collections, such as antique fire extinguishers and preserved human brains; a couple of spooky ghost stories; and a wealth of offbeat activities for you to try.

This book also reveals the secrets behind Indy icons you already know and love. Why does Holliday Park have its own "ancient" ruins? What surprises await inside the Indiana War Memorial and the City-County Building? Why does The Children's Museum have a collection of fossilized poop, and why does the Indiana State Museum display intricate Victorian artwork made from human hair?

For me, though, the greatest pleasure of writing this book has been telling the stories of the city's forgotten heroes: the lone woman who brought down the statewide Ku Klux Klan, for example, or the African American police officer whose murder was hushed up for seven decades. These voices deserve to be heard.

Writing this book taught me so much about the Circle City, from the quirks of its history to the delights of its present. With each new tidbit I learned, my love for this city deepened a little bit more. And I hope the same will be true for you, too.

1 A PARK THAT'S FOR THE BIRDS

What legacy did William Watson Woollen leave behind?

It's not easy to find Woolens Gardens. Or is it Woollen's Garden? Nobody can even agree on how it's spelled—that's how secret this park is. It has no signage, and to get there you'll have to ford Fall Creek. But you'll almost certainly have forty-three acres of forest all to yourself.

Attorney William Watson Woollen grew up on the property, then known as Buzzard's Roost, and he donated it to the city in 1909 with the stipulation that it remain in its natural state. An avid birdwatcher, he had recently published *Birds of Buzzard's Roost: One for Each Week, and Other Essays*, and he asked that the park be called Woollen's Garden of Birds and Botany. "It is an ideal place," Woollen wrote to the mayor at the time, according to Historic Indianapolis. "No other such beautiful and desirable place can be found within the same distance from the center of the city."

The property was declared a state nature preserve in 1987, and the parks department now maintains it as an untouched "natural resource area."

While we're here, let's settle the issue of the park's name. When Woollen founded the Indiana Nature Study Club in 1908, with forty charter members and annual dues of one dollar, the *Indianapolis Star* reported that most meetings would be held at Buzzard's Roost, the William Watson Woollen Garden of Birds

---

Woollen's Garden of Birds and Botany is connected to nearby Skiles Test Nature Park via a branch of the Fall Creek Parkway Trail.

Woollen's Garden of Birds and Botany is located just south of the Fall Creek Parkway Trail, on the opposite side of Fall Creek. Attorney William Watson Woollen donated the property to the city in 1909 with the stipulation that it be maintained in its natural state.

WOOLLEN'S GARDEN OF BIRDS AND BOTANY

WHAT A really, really hidden patch of wilderness

WHERE 6800 N. Fall Creek Rd.

COST Free

PRO TIP Ignore the address—it won't help you. Instead look for the small parking lot at 6846 East Fall Creek Parkway North Drive. From there the nature preserve is due south across Fall Creek. Maybe bring a canoe.

and Botany. The *Encyclopedia of Indianapolis* calls it Woollen's Garden of Birds and Botany, based on documentation from the Indiana Department of Natural Resources, and this echoes Woollen's own request. Officially, Indy Parks and Recreation calls it Woolens Gardens Park, which is obviously wrong because it misspells the name of the donor. So, despite the park's official name, this book refers to it in exactly the way Woollen intended.

2 A HEAD FOR MUSIC

Just what, exactly, is a Recordface?

"At first you never notice 'Recordface' street art, and then you see it everywhere," writes David Lindquist in his *Indianapolis Star* report about the city's strangest street art. And he's absolutely right—more than fifty (and counting) Recordface installations have been spotted around the city in the past several years. A Recordface consists of a vinyl record decorated to look like a face, with guitar picks for teeth and a red reflector for its single large eye. The hair is made from cassette tape. Each Recordface is "listening" to a small MP3 player, which always contains the same set of nine anonymous songs. But the MP3 players are often stolen, so you may see a Recordface hanging forlornly on a wall without its music.

Recordface isn't the official name; Lindquist made it up because the renegade artist is anonymous. Online it's also known as Vinyl Head and Black Vinyl. After the first article about the artwork appeared in the *Star*, Lindquist received a note apparently from the artist, who claimed the goal was just to make the world more interesting. "My intentions are respectful, passionate, and coming from a desire to mix street art, music, and Indiana geography," the note read.

Opinions differ on whether Recordface constitutes vandalism or guerilla art, and many of the installations are eventually removed. The ones attached to existing works of art, such as outdoor murals, have been particularly controversial. So

---

The Recordface playlist always contains the same nine electronic/hip-hop songs: Money, Trip, Poet or a Fool, Beauty 82, Juan, Monster Truck, Just You, Thank God, and Mrs. Bruer.

Meet Recordface, an unassuming guy with cassette-tape hair, a reflector eye, and guitar-pick teeth. For several years, an anonymous artist has been gluing Recordface heads to buildings all over the city, prompting a fierce debate about vandalism versus guerilla art.

RECORDFACE

WHAT Guerilla art or juvenile vandalism, depending on whom you ask

WHERE Throughout the city

COST Free

PRO TIP Carry a charger if you want to hear Recordface's favorite songs. If you're lucky enough to find a Recordface with its MP3 player still attached, it's likely that the battery is dead.

this book doesn't contain exact Recordface locations, but that's okay. You don't need to know exactly where to look. Once you're paying attention, Recordface will find you.

3 A FITTING TRIBUTE TO FIRE-FIGHTING

Which hidden museum houses nine hundred antique fire extinguishers?

Sometimes obscure museums are built around collections that, frankly, only the collectors themselves would ever find interesting. That is decidedly not the case with the Koorsen Fire Museum. This stunning tribute to the history of fire-fighting is unfortunately tucked away in an industrial park, and finding it requires wandering awkwardly through the offices of Koorsen Fire and Security. Go anyway.

The Koorsen Fire Museum houses about thirty antique fire engines, including a hand-pump model from 1840, a steam-powered engine from 1908, and a repurposed 1926 Ford Model T. About nine hundred antique fire extinguishers, made of brass, stainless steel, and copper, are fully restored and lined up in gleaming rows. Shelves near the entrance display "fire grenades," glass bottles of fire retardant that were designed to shatter when thrown into a fire. Other items on display include

KOORSEN FIRE MUSEUM

WHAT Every possible way to fight a fire

WHERE 2820 N. Webster Ave.

COST Free

PRO TIP The path to the museum is marked with arrows on signs throughout the office. When you pass the employee breakroom, you're almost there.

The oldest fire extinguisher in the Koorsen Fire Museum collection dates to 1789.

The Koorsen Fire Museum displays an astonishing array of fire-fighting equipment, including fire engines, strangely beautiful "fire grenades," and about nine hundred antique fire extinguishers.

fire alarms and pull boxes, leather fire buckets, fire-fighting masks, and even a fire-themed pinball game.

The collection is the life's work of Randy Koorsen, CEO, whose grandfather founded Koorsen Fire and Security in 1946. The company is now one of the nation's largest suppliers of fire extinguishers and related equipment, so hopefully the museum will have a home for many years to come.

4 A DINER WITH A DARK (CHOCOLATE) SECRET

Which vintage café has revived Indy's beloved Choc-Ola brand?

In 1961 a Peppy Grill opened in a promising location across the street from the thriving International Harvester foundry on Brookville Road. The small diner changed its name several times over the years, eventually becoming the Rock-Cola 1950s Café. International Harvester, meanwhile, became Navistar, and in 2015 the sprawling plant closed its doors. It has since been demolished, leaving the café all alone to face a barren stretch of industrial brownfields.

Most restaurants in those circumstances would have closed, but not the Rock-Cola 1950s Café. The vintage eatery still serves up all-day breakfast, burgers, and the staples of every true Hoosier diner: pork tenderloin sandwiches and sugar-cream pie.

The café evokes the spirit of the 1950s with pink walls, teal trim, and a black-and-white checkered floor. The booths and barstools are likewise upholstered in teal, and the walls are lined with Coca-Cola memorabilia, comic books, and photos of celebrities such as Marilyn Monroe and James Dean. Stapled to the ceiling are vintage movie posters and road signs.

Most importantly, the Rock-Cola 1950s Café is the only place where you can still order a Choc-Ola. The chocolate drink was

---

Choc-Ola inventor Harry Normington Sr. wanted to emphasize that the chocolatey drink contained milk, so he put a smiling cow on the label and coined the slogan "Cow Power."

At the Rock-Cola 1950s Café near Irvington, the walls and even the ceiling are lined with vintage memorabilia such as movie posters, comic books, road signs, and celebrity photos.

ROCK-COLA 1950s CAFÉ

WHAT The new official home of Choc-Ola

WHERE 5730 Brookville Rd.

COST Varies (budget friendly)

PRO TIP Gallon jugs of Choc-Ola are available for carryout.

manufactured in Indianapolis from 1944 to the early ’80s, when production was moved to Georgia and then slowly phased out. The brand had a series of owners, including Mott’s, but eventually the trademark was allowed to expire. Enter café owner Dan Iaria, who scooped up the trademark in 2010 and revived production the following year. The Rock-Cola 1950s Café is now the official home of this nostalgic Hoosier favorite, giving you a particularly sweet reason to seek out this hopping café in the middle of nowhere.

5 A RUN OF BAD LUCK

How did a historic Indy waterway simply vanish?

When Alexander Ralston laid out the Mile Square in 1821, his plan for the new city had one major flaw. The precise grid pattern was interrupted in the southeast corner by a stream called Pogue's Run. It entered the Mile Square at about East and Maryland streets, flowing southwest to the White River.

But contemporary Indy maps show no trace of Pogue's Run south of New York Street. So where did it go? For decades the stream was considered a public nuisance—an open sewer, a flood risk, and a breeding ground for mosquitos. In 1914, long before city planners understood the potential value of waterfront property, they simply funneled Pogue's Run underground into the storm sewers.

You can, technically speaking, walk or cycle the two miles of the Pogue's Run tunnel. It smells of sewage and is infested with giant rats and insects, and you'll be plunged into complete darkness not far from the entrance. You might run into graffiti artists or other nefarious characters. There's a confusing maze of side tunnels, and no cell service, so getting lost is risky. And the tunnel becomes extremely dangerous during rain, when high volumes of water rush through the narrow space. But if for some strange and reckless reason you still want to go, you'll find the entrance on the 1000 block of East New York Street, just east

---

Pogue's Run is named for one of the city's first white settlers, George Pogue, who arrived here with his family in 1819. In April 1821, he went in search of some lost (or perhaps stolen) horses and vanished without a trace.

The Pogue's Run tunnel, which runs for two miles underneath downtown Indianapolis, looks like the perfect setting for a horror movie. And director Dean Crow thought so, too. In 1988, he filmed a thriller here called Twice Under. *One review called it "among the worst 'movies' we've ever seen."*

of the interstate. There's a handy staircase to get you down the bank, and when the water level is low there are concrete pathways along the sides of the tunnel.

THE POGUE'S RUN TUNNEL

WHAT A creepy (and very dangerous) underground adventure

WHERE Entrance on East New York Street, immediately east of the railroad tracks, in the parking lot between Arrow Powder Coating (1045 E. Vermont Ave.) and Accessa (1034 E. New York St.)

COST Free

NOTEWORTHY The Pogue's Run tunnel makes appearances in two recent novels set in Indianapolis: *Underground Airlines* by Ben H. Winters and *Turtles All the Way Down* by John Green.

6 A TIME-HONORED TRADITION

Which local shop houses a museum of *Doctor Who* memorabilia?

Any Time Lord can tell you that the BBC launched *Doctor Who* in 1963, making it the longest-running sci-fi series in history. For nearly seven decades, various Doctors (thirteen in all) have traveled the universe in the TARDIS, using their sonic screwdrivers to battle enemies such as Daleks and Weeping Angels. The show is a staple of British popular culture and has a worldwide cult following—but it's still a bit surprising to find a huge *Doctor Who* store and museum right here in Central Indiana.

When Keith Bradbury founded Who North America back in 1998, it was hard to find *Doctor Who* merchandise on this side of the Atlantic, and the company served a huge untapped market of US fans. But even in the era of Amazon, Who North America is still one of the nation's largest retailers of *Doctor Who* toys, games, accessories, DVDs, books, collectibles, and more. Unusual finds include Dalek-shaped soap and TARDIS-themed dinnerware, towels, piggy banks, teapots, Christmas stockings, and umbrellas.

Bradbury opened the current location in 2016, setting aside half of the building as a museum for *Doctor Who* collectibles,

---

The Time Lord of *Doctor Who* travels in a time machine called the TARDIS (Time and Relative Dimension in Space). It may look like a small British police callbox, but I hear it's bigger on the inside.

In the long-running Doctor Who *series, the Time Lord uses his sonic screwdriver to battle enemies such as Cybermen and Daleks. Both antagonists are on display at Who North America, a* Doctor Who *shop and museum located in Camby.*

WHO NORTH AMERICA

WHAT An homage to a legendary sci-fi series

WHERE 8901 S. State Road 67, Camby

COST Free

PRO TIP Who North America stocks several hard-to-find British treats, including Jammie Dodgers and Jelly Babies.

including rare items from the 1960s. After you peruse the glass cases of memorabilia, try the *Doctor Who* pinball game and get a photo with the TARDIS, a Dalek, a Cyberman, or life-sized cardboard cutouts of various Doctors and their companions. Or, you can simply hang out and watch whichever of the 850 *Doctor Who* episodes the shop has on TV.

7 A BREATH OF FRESH AIR

Why does an Indy hospital have a rooftop garden?

Eskenazi Health offers a decidedly unexpected amenity to its patients, visitors, and staff. Atop the outpatient care center is the Sky Farm, a rooftop garden with wonderful views of the downtown skyline.

The Sky Farm offers much more than scenic views, however. The first rooftop hospital garden in the nation, it often serves as a relaxing escape from the stresses of the hospital. And it's an integral part of the hospital's "healing environment." The terrace spans thirty-five thousand square feet, of which five thousand square feet is growing space. The sky farmer (yes, that's her actual title) raises sixty varieties of fruits, vegetables, and flowers, harvesting more than three thousand pounds of produce each year. Some of that produce makes its way to the café salad bar, but most is used for cooking classes, nutrition seminars, and other educational programs. The gift shop uses the flowers to make bouquets.

The Sky Farm got a makeover in 2019, including new ground pavers and fencing. But the primary goal was adding more raised planting beds, which provide easier access for patients in wheelchairs or with other mobility issues. A hospital may be a sterile environment, but sometimes to truly heal you have to get your hands dirty.

THE SKY FARM

WHAT A secret garden with a view

WHERE Eskenazi Health, 720 Eskenazi Ave.

COST Free

PRO TIP To access the Sky Farm, take the green elevators to the seventh floor.

The Sky Farm at Eskenazi Health produces more than three thousand pounds of fruits, vegetables, and flowers each year. The garden is open to the public around the clock and provides stunning views of the downtown skyline. Photos courtesy Eskenazi Health.

Running the Sky Farm at Eskenazi Health is not without challenges. The wind is stronger up there, so some plants require extra stakes, and the soil dries out (and sometimes freezes) more quickly than usual.

8 THE LINGERIE LEGACY

Why does one Mass Ave walkway smell so good?

The weirdest piece of public art in the Massachusetts Avenue Cultural District is also the least conspicuous: an underground scent machine. Tucked away in an alley on the 700 block of Mass Ave, *Chatham Passage*—by conceptual artist Sean Derry—is an underground concrete vault topped with an elaborate steel grate. Inside the vault are LED lights and a machine that spreads the scent of English roses.

Installed in 2010, the artwork pays homage to the history of the area. The Real Silk Hosiery Mill opened here in 1922, manufacturing intimate apparel such as hosiery, underwear, and lingerie. The scent of roses is meant to convey the same atmosphere of intimacy and luxury. The mill closed in the 1950s, but the building still exists (it has, of course, been converted into condos).

Don't miss the many other public art installations along Mass Ave. Favorites include the digital *Ann Dancing* sign by Julian Opie, a giant head sculpture called *Brickhead 3*, and enormous murals of several Indianapolis writers. The *Care/Don't Care* installation by Indy artist Jamie Pawlus looks just like a "walk/don't walk" sign, so it blends easily into the scenery, and some pedestrians don't even notice it. (Look closely at the intersection of College Avenue and St. Clair Street.)

The Indy Arts Guide (indyartsguide.org) maintains an online directory of public art that you can search by medium, artist, neighborhood, and several other categories. Scavenger hunt, anyone?

A strange piece of public art hides in plain sight in an alley off Mass Ave. The piece, called Chatham Passage, *consists of a scent machine nestled in an underground vault. Photo courtesy Visit Indy.*

CHATHAM PASSAGE

WHAT A kooky art installation with a scent machine

WHERE The alley next to Metro Nightclub, 707 Massachusetts Ave.

COST Free

PRO TIP *Chatham Passage* is located along the Indianapolis Cultural Trail, a unique pedestrian pathway connecting the city's designated cultural districts. Walk, run, or cycle the trail to find many other pieces of public art.

9 A FASHIONABLE ADDRESS

Why did Hollywood celebrities flock to an Indianapolis cottage?

In the early 1900s, George and Nellie Meier were at the center of the city's social scene. George was a fashion designer with an international reputation, and Nellie was famous for palm-reading, which she called "scientific palmistry."

In 1910, the couple bought a small bungalow on North Pennsylvania Street, calling it Tuckaway because it was tucked into a grove of trees. They could have afforded a much grander residence, but they immediately fell in love with the Meridian Park home. After completing renovations—which included lifting off the entire roof, adding a second story, and plopping the roof back on—the couple began throwing the parties for which they became famous. Over the years, their guests included Albert Einstein, Eleanor Roosevelt, Walt Disney, Amelia Earhart, Joan Crawford, and countless others. The gatherings sometimes included impromptu concerts by George Gershwin or Sergei Rachmaninoff, or dance performances by Isadora Duncan.

One legend connected with the house concerns the actress Carole Lombard. An Indiana native, Lombard visited Indianapolis in 1942 to headline a rally for the sale of war bonds. According to the story, Lombard visited Nellie for a palm-reading that day, and Nellie—sensing grave danger—warned Lombard not to travel. But Lombard shrugged off the warning, and she died in a plane crash the very next day.

In 1937, Nellie Meier published a book about her palm-reading exploits. Titled *Lions' Paws: The Story of Famous Hands*, it quickly became a bestseller.

The legendary parties at Tuckaway, the Indianapolis home of George and Nellie Meier, sometimes included impromptu performances by George Gershwin or Sergei Rachmaninoff. The couple's celebrity friends included Franklin and Eleanor Roosevelt, Walt Disney, Albert Einstein, and the era's most popular film stars. Photo courtesy the Indiana Historical Society, P0060.

TUCKAWAY

WHAT A house with a star-studded history

WHERE 3128 N. Pennsylvania St.

COST Not open to the public

PRO TIP Although Tuckaway is a private residence, the owners often open the house to visitors during neighborhood home tours.

After George and Nellie died, the house passed to their niece, a dancer named Ruth Cannon. She lived at Tuckaway until 1968, but after she moved the house sat vacant and fell into disrepair. Fortunately, the home eventually cast its spell on Ken Keene, who purchased it in 1972 and carefully restored it to its former glory. Now the home is owned by historic-restoration experts Joe Everhart and Ken Ramsay and is listed on the National Register of Historic Places.

10 AN EVENING ON THE ICE

What sports lesson starts with how to fall down?

Did you know you could win an Olympic gold medal for sweeping ice and delivering stones? That's the wacky lingo of curling, a low-key sport that people notice only once every four years, during the Winter Olympics. And even then the sport is overshadowed by flashier competitions on the ice, such as figure skating and hockey. The curlers don't even wear ice skates.

Curling originated on the frozen lakes of Scotland, hundreds of years ago, and is one of the world's oldest team sports. Yet it didn't become an official Olympic sport until 1998, at the games in Nagano, Japan. Confused viewers have been trying to figure out the rules ever since.

Fortunately, the Circle City Curling Club can alleviate that confusion. The club operates leagues for players of all skill levels, and it also runs introductory curling clinics. You'll spend the first half hour learning the rules and basic safety procedures, including the proper way to fall so you don't spend the evening in the emergency room. Then you'll head out on the ice with a coach and play some "ends," getting hands-on experience with launching stones, sweeping, scoring, and planning your strategy. You may not make the next Olympic team, but at least you'll understand what you're seeing on TV.

You will fall, and so will everyone else. But not as much as you might expect—the surface of the ice will be "pebbled" to help control the speed of the stones.

The Circle City Curling Club's introductory clinics are a crash course—sometimes literally—in the rules, techniques, and strategies of curling. Photo courtesy Susan Fleck.

CIRCLE CITY CURLING CLUB

WHAT Curling lessons for the absolute beginner

WHERE Varies

COST $40

PRO TIP These clinics often sell out, so book well in advance.

Dress for the cold of the ice rink, but be prepared to shed layers as the activity heats up. You'll also need a second pair of shoes, preferably with rubber soles. Dirt and debris on the ice can divert even the most carefully aimed stone, so you'll be asked to change into clean shoes before stepping onto the ice.

11 INDIANA'S WEIRDEST ROADSIDE ATTRACTION

Why does a small Indiana town have a giant ball of paint?

The World's Largest Ball of Paint started its life as an ordinary baseball. But it now has a circumference of fourteen feet and weighs a whopping five thousand pounds. Over four decades, Mike and Glenda Carmichael, their son, and thousands of visitors have added more than twenty-six thousand coats of paint. The ball hangs from an industrial-strength hook in its own custom barn in Alexandria, Indiana, and it has held the Guinness World Record for "most layers in a ball of paint" since 2004.

Mike Carmichael created his first ball of paint in the 1960s, when he worked a summer job at a hardware store. One day he knocked over a can of paint while playing catch with a friend, and the mess made Carmichael curious. What would the ball look like with a thousand layers of paint? That early experiment was eventually donated to a children's home. But a few years after their son was born, the Carmichaels decided to start over with a new baseball. They brushed on the first coat on New Year's Day 1977, and the ball has been growing steadily ever since—although now the Carmichaels use long-handled paint rollers rather than brushes.

You too can add a layer to the World's Largest Ball of Paint; just call ahead and make an appointment. You can even choose your

---

The most popular paint colors for the World's Largest Ball of Paint are yellow, blue, and green, each with several thousand layers. The least popular, each with just a handful of layers, are maroon, silver, and lilac.

The World's Largest Ball of Paint started its life as a baseball. More than 26,000 coats of paint later, the ball weighs five thousand pounds and has a circumference of fourteen feet. It has held the Guinness World Record since 2004.

WORLD'S LARGEST BALL OF PAINT

WHAT A baseball coated in 26,000 (and counting) layers of paint

WHERE 10696 N. 200 W., Alexandria

COST Free (donations accepted)

PRO TIP Call (765) 724-4088 to make an appointment.

own color, provided that it differs from the previous layer. The Carmichaels keep meticulous records of every layer, including the date, paint color, and name and hometown of the painter, and as a keepsake they'll give you a certificate showing which layer you painted. There's no fee to paint the ball, but consider making a small donation to cover the cost of the paint.

12 THE WHALING WALL

Why does landlocked Indy have a giant ocean mural?

In 1981, muralist Robert Wyland embarked on a public art project that would eventually span five continents and thirteen countries—one of the largest public art projects in history. For nearly three decades, he traveled the globe painting huge public murals of whales and other sea creatures in their marine habitats. The goal, he said, was to raise public awareness of marine conservation issues.

Indianapolis is home to the seventy-fourth "Wyland Wall," which was dedicated in 1997. Titled *Orcas Passage*, it spans 153 feet by 35 feet on the north wall of the John Morton-Finney Center for Educational Services. The location is less than ideal; one-way traffic on nearby Delaware Street runs north as well, so commuters can drive past the mural every day without even knowing it's there.

In fact, Wyland originally chose the five-story wall of 7 East Washington Street. But that wall is home to *The Runners*, a 1975 mural by James McQuiston. Wyland said the

ORCAS PASSAGE BY ROBERT WYLAND

WHAT A conservation-minded mural with a controversial past

WHERE 120 E. Walnut St.

COST Free

NOTEWORTHY *Indianapolis Monthly* once described Robert Wyland as "sort of like Thomas Kinkade, except with cetaceans."

James McQuiston's mural, *The Runners*, was added to the Washington Street cityscape after the design won a 1975 contest sponsored by the parks department and the Greater Indianapolis Progress Committee.

Painted by Robert Wyland, the Orcas Passage *mural is part of an international series designed to get people thinking about environmental issues. Wyland originally planned to paint over James McQuiston's mural on Washington Street,* The Runners, *but a public outcry forced him to select a different wall.*

mural was "deteriorating into an eyesore" and had no qualms about painting over it. But McQuiston organized a letter-writing campaign to save his mural, and Wyland's choice was overruled by public opinion. More than two decades later, Wyland's mural is largely forgotten, and McQuiston's mural endures as one of the city's most adorable works of art.

13 THE HOUSE OF BLUE LIGHTS

What's the truth behind Indy's favorite urban legend?

Here are the facts: Born in 1889, Skiles Test was the heir to an automotive fortune. As an adult, the eccentric millionaire bought a large estate northeast of the city and filled the property with oddities: a small railway network, a motorized surfboard, underground tunnels, and even a pet cemetery.

Test also built his own power plant on the property. (That's one way to settle a dispute with the power company.) That electricity kept the property glowing with blue lights—Test's favorite color—including strings of blue Christmas lights during the holidays and blue pool lights that were reflected and magnified by the home's exterior white tiles.

In the 1940s, rumors began to spread that Test's wife had died mysteriously. The grief-stricken millionaire had refused to bury her, the rumor claimed, instead placing her in a glass coffin that he propped upright in the living room. Several generations of Indianapolis teenagers, dared by friends to creep up to the house and peek in the windows, swore they'd seen her there—dressed all in blue.

The only problem with the story: Test's wife wasn't dead. "In truth, his wife and two ex-wives long outlived him," writes Ryan Hamlett for Historic Indianapolis. At first, Test was amused by the story of the House of Blue Lights, but he eventually became frustrated by the trespassing and vandalism on the property.

Skiles Test employed a full-time veterinarian to care for his many pets, including about 150 cats.

The House of Blue Lights no longer exists, but the property on which it stood is now the Skiles Test Nature Park. According to urban legend, the forest still sometimes glows with eerie and inexplicable blue lights.

SKILES TEST NATURE PARK

WHAT A forest with a ghostly secret

WHERE 6828 Fall Creek Rd.

COST Free

PRO TIP The eighty-acre nature park has several miles of paved and unpaved trails, offering a serene escape from the city.

Test died in 1964 and was buried in Crown Hill Cemetery. The estate auction drew a crowd of nearly fifty thousand people, all hoping to catch a glimpse of a glass coffin that didn't exist. The city now maintains the property as Skiles Test Nature Park, and the house is long gone. But at night, ghost hunters claim, the forest still glows with blue light.

14 A CURIOUS COSTUME CONTEST

When is a baked potato actually a llama in disguise?

Every August, nearly a million people attend the Indiana State Fair, primarily for its midway, concerts, and concession stands. But at its heart the fair is about Indiana agriculture, and fair organizers take that subject seriously. But there is one notable exception: the llama costume contest.

This bizarre annual event showcases llamas (or alpacas) and their owners dressed in matching costumes. Themes have included everything from Muppets and Dr. Seuss characters to pirates and penguins. Llamas have even made appearances as dragons, piñatas, tow trucks, and baked potatoes. To be fair, the contest isn't *completely* superfluous. One of the judging criteria is the difficulty level of training the animal to "accept and exhibit" that particular costume.

The Indiana State Fair also offers prizes for the most artistic scarecrow, the most enormous pumpkin, the prettiest marbles and buttons, the best fair-themed LEGO sculpture, and various categories of "decorative vegetable art." In that context, maybe a llama costume contest isn't so strange after all.

Llamas in disguise aren't the only quirky sight at the Indiana State Fair. The list includes a giant cheese sculpture, a seed-spitting contest, daredevil lumberjack demonstrations, and a Spam-themed cooking competition.

LLAMA COSTUME CONTEST

WHAT A prize for the best-disguised pack animal

WHERE Indiana State Fairgrounds, 1202 E. Thirty-Eighth St.

COST Free with fair admission ($13)

NOTEWORTHY Fair leaders once envisioned the Walk of Legends, a Hoosier version of the Hollywood Walk of Fame. John Mellencamp and Orville Redenbacher were among the celebrities who signed their names in concrete, but the slabs have been moved several times and are largely forgotten. Look for them along the northeast and northwest walk tunnels.

Top: Ella White of Fort Wayne and her llama, Mist, chose a Star Wars theme for the 2017 Indiana State Fair. Photo courtesy Leslie White. Bottom: Meagan Earley of Greencastle and her llama, Razzle Dazzle, show off the ribbon for their Toy Story costumes at the 2018 Indiana State Fair. Photo courtesy Kristen Earley.

15 A MUSEUM THAT TAKES LIBERTIES

Why does Indy have a Statue of Liberty museum?

The Teeny Statue of Liberty Museum is exactly what it sounds like—a very small museum dedicated to Lady Liberty. It is curated by Tim Harmon, who co-owns the salvage shop two doors down, Tim and Julie's Another Fine Mess. More than thirty years ago, Harmon was working a salvage job when he came across some shipping boxes with the Statue of Liberty printed on the side. He liked the idea that a box with her image might show up anywhere in the world, so he saved one. Later, on a salvage job at an abandoned school, he found a cache of Statue of Liberty erasers in a teacher's desk. Harmon took it as a sign, and the collection grew from there. It now includes about five hundred items. "We don't buy anything on eBay," said co-owner Julie Crow on a recent tour. "We wait to see what comes to us." Some items have turned up on additional salvage jobs, and others have been gifts from family members and friends. Even complete strangers have been known to donate items.

The collection includes some things you might expect: posters, books, shot glasses, postcards, t-shirts, decorative plates, coffee mugs, and dozens of souvenir statuettes. But you might be surprised by the Statue of Liberty wind-up toys, lamps, toothbrush holders, and lawn sprinklers. There's a limited-edition Statue of Liberty Barbie wearing a red, white, and blue gown

---

Tim and Julie's Another Fine Mess is a fascinating maze of architectural salvage, from doorknobs and electrical fittings to commercial signage and antique cash registers.

A Lady Liberty wind-up toy is one of many strange objects at the Teeny Statue of Liberty Museum on Tenth Street. The collection, which started with a cardboard box and some erasers, now includes about five hundred items.

TEENY STATUE OF LIBERTY MUSEUM

WHAT An homage to Lady Liberty

WHERE 2907 E. Tenth St.

COST Fifty cents

PRO TIP If the door is locked, pop into the salvage shop to request a tour.

designed by Bob Mackie. Miss Piggy and the Ms. Green M&M character also make appearances as Lady Liberty. And don't forget to look up: Harmon has compensated for the small space by stapling some of his memorabilia to the ceiling.

16 A CHAMBER OF SECRETS

Which overlooked architectural gem is packed with symbolic surprises?

The Indiana State Library was founded in 1825, making it the oldest state agency you've never heard of. Originally a reference library for state employees and elected officials, it has been open to the public for more than a century. And that's fortunate, because the beautiful downtown building contains some secrets worth exploring.

Start your tour outside the 1934 building, which features the stripped-down classical architecture of the period. Exterior carvings depict the "makers of the state," such as explorers and farmers; the liberal arts, such as history and philosophy; and the "builders of Indiana," such as a Native American, a woodsman, and a trapper.

Inside, bronze floor medallions depict the coins of many nations, but seven are mysteriously missing. "We have no idea what was removed, or why," writes Steven J. Schmidt in his comprehensive book *The Architectural Treasures of the Indiana State Library*. The first floor houses a small exhibition hall, the genealogy division, and the Indiana Historical Bureau. Upstairs are several reading rooms and the great hall, where you'll find an honest-to-goodness card catalog containing 1,482 drawers and nearly a million cards.

The entire building is rich with symbolism, starting with the construction materials: Indiana walnut, limestone, and sandstone. Stained-glass windows and murals by J. Scott

---

In the lobby of the Indiana State Library, a plaque memorializes the pioneers who "had the wisdom and foresight to provide for the self-instruction" of the state's future citizens.

The great hall of the Indiana State Library has an actual card catalog, along with stained-glass windows, a barrel-vaulted ceiling, and bronze chandeliers designed to look like cornstalks.

INDIANA STATE LIBRARY

WHAT A historic building steeped in symbolism

WHERE 315 W. Ohio St.

COST Free

NOTEWORTHY The scene depicted in the central stained-glass window is the Indiana constitutional convention of 1816.

Williams depict scenes from Indiana history, and the bronze chandeliers were inspired by cornstalks. The many owl images symbolize wisdom. And several of the ceilings are decorated with historical printers' marks. Indianapolis was once home to the Bobbs-Merrill Publishing Company, an industry giant, but its mark is strangely absent—allegedly because of a spat between the publisher and the head librarian at the time.

17 AN OASIS OF COMFORT FOOD

THE OASIS DINER

WHAT A restaurant with a penchant for travel

WHERE 405 W. Main St., Plainfield

COST Varies (budget friendly)

PRO TIP Try the "Kansas City" breakfast—house-made biscuits smothered in sausage gravy and topped with two eggs, crumbled bacon, and melted cheddar cheese.

How did a historic diner get from Six Points to Plainfield?

When we say a restaurant has "arrived" in Indiana, we usually mean that a national chain has opened its first location here. But when the Oasis Diner "arrived" in Indiana in 1954, the meaning was more literal: the restaurant showed up on a train from New Jersey (some assembly required). The gleaming stainless-steel diner soon became a local favorite. But that wasn't the end of its journey.

For decades the diner did brisk business on US 40 between Indianapolis and Plainfield, in a small community called Six Points. It had a string of owners over the years, but it always served all-day breakfast and breaded pork tenderloins. Beginning in the 1990s, however, the Six Points neighborhood was gradually overtaken by the industrial sprawl surrounding the Indianapolis International Airport. The Oasis closed down in 2008, and in 2009 the historic structure was condemned.

In a way, that turned out to be good news for the Oasis. Indiana Landmarks included the diner on its 2010 list of the ten

---

Shiny prefab diners once lined US 40 (the National Road) all across the country. In Indiana, the Oasis is the only survivor.

The cars have changed, and the outdoor seating is new. But otherwise it's hard to tell the difference between the Oasis Diner of yesteryear and the restored version of today. Photos courtesy Oasis Diner.

most endangered historic buildings in the state. And that caught the attention of Plainfield officials, who thought the diner was a perfect fit for the town's revitalized historic district. In 2014, after a complicated planning process, the Oasis was loaded onto a flatbed semi for the four-mile journey to Plainfield.

Since then, owners Doug Huff and Don Rector have carefully restored the diner to its original look. Breads and pastries are now made in-house, and a few modern dishes have crept onto the menu. But the restaurant still serves all-day breakfast, including a breaded pork tenderloin topped with rich sausage gravy.

18 A GALLERY OF GRAFFITI

Who's behind all that street art in Fountain Square?

In its grittier years, the Fountain Square neighborhood was a low-rent enclave for the city's starving artists. Now the spruced-up cultural district is home to some of the city's best restaurants and nightlife options. Even the neighborhood's legendary graffiti has gone upscale—now it's called street art—and the side streets and back alleys are an ever-changing outdoor gallery.

Start your tour in the parking lot behind New Day Craft, 1102 Prospect Street, where you'll find a wacky robot painted by Devious. The giant bulldog, named Frenchie, is a tribute to late graffiti artist Speedbeard. And the local "Infamous with Style" graffiti crew—Dose, Sacred317, 6Cents, and Detour—painted a gold medallion here to celebrate its twentieth anniversary. Across Shelby Street, in the alley running northwest to Woodlawn Avenue, look for an angry brown monster and a large portrait of Björk. The Fabulous Aerosol Brothers (FAB) Crew, a collaboration between 6Cents and Sacred317, is responsible for the dancer in the green dress.

At 1043 Virginia Avenue, check out the memorial mural to late *Indianapolis Star* photojournalist Mpozi Mshale Tolbert. The dandelion mural next to it is part of the Lilly Oncology on Canvas program, which underwrites works by artists with cancer.

The graffiti in the rear parking lot of Dance Sophisticates, 1605 Prospect Street, was created during the 2013 Subsurface Graffiti Expo. The FAB Crew organized the annual event in Fountain Square for more than a decade, but in 2016 the crew suspended

---

The 200 block of Shelby Street is another popular graffiti gallery, especially along the train tracks. (Be careful!)

Start your tour of Fountain Square's legendary street art with this purple robot in the parking lot behind New Day Craft. Devious, a graffiti artist based in Cincinnati, painted the robot during the 2012 Subsurface Graffiti Expo.

future events because, it claimed, gentrification was driving demand for professional murals rather than graffiti, and the community was "looking for more than dope lettering." Go see what remains of their dope lettering while you still can.

FOUNTAIN SQUARE STREET ART

WHAT An unofficial gallery of graffiti

WHERE Fountain Square neighborhood

COST Free

PRO TIP You'll find sanctioned FAB Crew murals all over town now—in corporate conference rooms, on restaurant walls, and even on IndyGo buses. Check out the crew's online portfolio (fabcrew.com) and see how many you can track down.

19 A PARK WITH A PURPOSE

Which greenspace has the city's strangest view?

Indianapolis is the nation's largest city not located on a navigable body of water, so the interstate system that crisscrosses the city has been essential to its economic success. But building highways through the city has also created enormous concrete barriers between (and within) existing neighborhoods. One of the most painful divisions occurred about forty years ago, when I-65/I-70 divided Fletcher Place and Holy Rosary from neighboring Fountain Square. The new Indianapolis Cultural Trail has reconnected the neighborhoods, to some extent, but residents still wanted a place where they could meet in the middle.

That's the origin story for a truly bizarre park, a greenspace called The Idle: A Point of View that opened in 2018. Located between the divided neighborhoods, the small park has its own version of a scenic overlook—a view of the two highways' south split. People for Urban Progress stocked the park with orange seats salvaged from Bush Stadium, so visitors can relax and watch the traffic flow. It's more entertaining than it sounds: *Indianapolis Monthly* called the park "a surprising, creative, resourceful, original, and practical use" of what is essentially a highway median.

The runner-up for Indy's weirdest park is the Park of the Laments, located within 100 Acres: The Virginia B. Fairbanks Art and Nature Park. The entrance is a dark, narrow tunnel lined with stones, but a secret garden awaits you inside.

Located along the Indianapolis Cultural Trail, a new greenspace called The Idle: A Point of View has a unique and unexpected scenic overlook. At the entrance, a John Lennon song lyric branded into the cement reads "Sitting here watching the wheels go round and round."

THE IDLE: A POINT OF VIEW

WHAT An urban park with a unique perspective

WHERE Virginia Avenue between the I-65/I-70 bridges

COST Free

PRO TIP The Idle was the brainchild of Tom Battista, who owns the nearby Bluebeard restaurant. Stop by for an ever-changing seasonal menu, clever cocktails, and the city's best bread pudding.

Neighborhood residents spent five long years cutting through bureaucratic red tape and securing funding to get the park built. A bench in the park is carved with a quote that seems emblematic of their efforts: "When I came here, I was looking for a community. Then I realized I was helping to create one."

20 A NIGHT AT THE MOVIES

Where can you find the city's only drive-in theater?

Sure, modern movie theaters have reclining seats, surround-sound stereo systems, and "choose your own flavor" soda machines. But with expensive tickets and overpriced concessions, a night at the movies now costs a small fortune.

In contrast, the Tibbs Drive-In Theatre is an absolute bargain. Each screen shows two movies per night, one at dusk and one closer to midnight, but you only have to pay admission once. So stop arguing with your date about whether to see a romantic comedy or the latest superhero movie—at Tibbs, you both win.

You *could* watch the movie from your front seat, but don't. Veteran Tibbs customers arrive early and tailgate, setting up folding chairs in front of their cars. Moviegoers with SUVs convert their trunks into seating areas with piles of blankets and cushions, and customers with trucks sometimes arrive with actual sofas.

The concession stand has a wider selection than usual. In addition to popcorn and candy, you'll find pizzas, burgers, pork tenderloin sandwiches, and ice cream. But Tibbs also allows you to bring your own food and drinks—another reason why this theater is such a bargain. There's even a playground in case the kids need to burn off the sugar high.

For more nostalgic fun, try Mug-n-Bun (5211 W. Tenth St.). The drive-in is known for pork tenderloin sandwiches and its house-brewed root beer, which is available by the gallon for carryout.

At the Tibbs Drive-in Theatre, sound is transmitted via FM radio, with a different frequency for each of the four screens. If you're planning a tailgate-style viewing party, be sure to bring a portable radio.

TIBBS DRIVE-IN THEATRE

WHAT A nostalgic entertainment bargain

WHERE 480 S. Tibbs Ave.

COST $11 for adults, $6 for kids

PRO TIP The theater closes for the winter, generally reopening in early March.

Located on the southwest side, Tibbs opened in 1967 with just one screen, adding two more in 1972 and a fourth in 1999. Indianapolis once had more than a dozen drive-in theaters, but this family-owned gem is the only survivor. Coming here is more than just a night at the movies; it's an experience you'll never forget.

21 THE SUPREME SACRIFICE

Why was the shooting death of an Indianapolis police officer virtually ignored?

In November 1998, more than two hundred people attended a memorial service at Crown Hill Cemetery for a policeman who had died in the line of duty. But there was something unusual about the service: the officer in question had been dead for more than seventy-five years.

The officer was William Whitfield, who was shot while on duty in 1922. Then, as now, the death of a police officer was usually front-page news. Flags would be flown at half-mast, and government officials would release statements condemning the violence. But Whitfield received no such attention, and there was no manhunt for his killer—because Whitfield was African American. He was buried in an unmarked grave at Crown Hill Cemetery, without any of the usual ceremony.

In *Legends in Blue: Selected Stories from the History of the Indianapolis Police Department*, police historian Wayne Sharp speculates that Whitfield's death was in fact an assassination. In the highly segregated city, the African American officer had been assigned to patrol a white neighborhood, and his shooting may have been intended to deliver a message.

Fortunately, that's not where the story ends. In 1998, Sharp wrote an article about Whitfield for the Indianapolis Police Department's internal newsletter. Officers who read it

---

The city's first police department was established in 1854. But officers soon infuriated the public by attempting to actually enforce a local prohibition law, and the entire police force was disbanded.

This headstone at Crown Hill Cemetery honors Indianapolis Police Department patrolman William Whitfield, the first African American IPD officer to be killed in the line of duty. His sacrifice was largely ignored at the time of his death, and his grave remained unmarked for seventy-six years.

THE GRAVE OF WILLIAM WHITFIELD

WHAT A long-overdue memorial to a fallen officer

WHERE Crown Hill Cemetery, 700 W. Thirty-Eighth St. (Section F, Plot 7056)

COST Free

NOTEWORTHY Crown Hill Cemetery is the final resting place of both cops and robbers, including legendary gangster John Dillinger.

immediately began collecting donations for a gravestone, reaching their goal in just three hours. When the stone was placed a few months later, the memorial service finally included honor guard ceremonies and a twenty-one-gun salute. The stone reads: “Patrolman William Whitfield, 1885–1922. First black officer to make the supreme sacrifice in the line of duty.”

22 CULTURAL IMPERIALISM

Where can you buy a limited-edition mead flavored with espresso?

You don't have to be at a shopping mall to fight the crowds on Black Friday. Simply head to Fountain Square, where New Day Craft releases its limited-edition Imperial Breakfast Magpie each year at high noon. The line starts forming around 7 a.m., but the atmosphere is more like a tailgate. New Day hands out free Long's Bakery doughnuts, and customers bring along rare beers, meads, and ciders to share while waiting.

New Day Craft's specialty is mead, or honey-based wine. The Imperial Breakfast Magpie is a black raspberry mead, infused with locally roasted espresso and aged in bourbon barrels for fourteen months. The unusual—but delicious—flavor includes notes of coffee, chocolate, berries, and oak.

The limit for each customer is just one case, but the Magpie sells out anyway. Your next chance is later in the winter, when New Day sometimes releases Magpie variants with flavors such as vanilla or cacao cinnamon.

Year-round meads on the New Day menu include Washington's Folly (tart cherry), Rethinker (dry hopped blueberry), Shelby Blue Ribbon (strawberry and rhubarb), and Live Currant (black currant). The meadery is also known for its hard ciders, which are infused with natural sweeteners such as

---

Your Hoosier bucket list should also include Dark Lord Day, the annual release party in Munster, Indiana, for 3 Floyds Brewing's Dark Lord Russian-Style Imperial Stout. Tickets are $180 each but still sell out quickly.

Customers line up outside New Day Craft on Black Friday to buy a case of Imperial Breakfast Magpie. The limited-edition seasonal brew is a black raspberry mead infused with espresso and aged in bourbon barrels for more than a year. Photos courtesy New Day Craft.

TAPPING THE IMPERIAL BREAKFAST MAGPIE

WHAT A boozy Black Friday sale

WHERE New Day Craft, 1102 Prospect St.

COST Free (plus a budget for your Magpie)

PRO TIP Bring a lawn chair and remember to bundle up for the weather.

honey and sorghum. There's also a new line of mead spritzers. You can try them all with tasting flights at the Fountain Square tasting room, where special events include chair massages, yoga classes, henna tattooing sessions, live music, and art exhibitions.

23 TWISTED TRESSES

Where can you see jewelry made from human hair?

The Victorians were a sentimental bunch, and many of their elaborate mourning rituals now seem strange to us. Take, for example, the habit of posing for photographs with the bodies of recently deceased loved ones. But perhaps the strangest was the art of "hair work," using a dead person's hair to create mementos such as jewelry and memorial wreaths. As the book *Ladies' Fancywork* pointed out in 1876, "the hair is the only part of our beloved friends which can be kept *in memoriam*," and therefore it was only natural to "preserve the treasure in some way that will testify our appreciation of its value."

VICTORIAN HAIR WORK

WHAT Artwork made from the locks of loved ones

WHERE Indiana State Museum, 650 W. Washington St.

COST $17 for adults, $12 for kids

PRO TIP Spend a few minutes at the museum watching the mesmerizing swing of the Foucault pendulum. Its clockwise movement completes a full circle every thirty-seven hours, showing the rotation of Earth on its axis.

Hoosier examples of Victorian hair work are on display at the Indiana State Museum as part of an exhibit of funerary artifacts. Objects made from human hair include a bracelet, a watch chain, a floral bouquet, and several memorial wreaths. Although wreaths made with hair from one person were generally signs of mourning, the Victorians also created "family trees" using hair from multiple family members, both living and dead. (One such "tree" in the museum collection uses hair from twenty-five different people.) The pieces may be haunting and strange, but they are also intricate, beautiful, and skillfully made—perhaps because of the tips in *Ladies' Fancywork*.

Shelby County resident Amanda Snyder Snepp created this framed hair wreath in the early 1880s. It incorporates both horsehair and hair samples from all her family members. Photo courtesy Indiana State Museum and Historic Sites.

Between 1842 and 1866, Franklin County resident Esther Hall Hyde created this floral bouquet using the hair of her twelve children. Photo courtesy Indiana State Museum and Historic Sites.

Other quirky highlights at the Indiana State Museum include Ernie Pyle's typewriter, Bobby Plump's basketball goal, and the actual mallet that Abraham Lincoln used for splitting rails.

24 A FRIENDLY RETREAT

Which Indy church created a forest for meditation?

From its inception, the Religious Society of Friends has embraced the concept of silent, meditative worship. Quaker meetings often exemplify Psalm 46:10, which begins "Be still and know that I am God." Although traditions have changed over the years, Indianapolis First Friends still offers some of these "unprogrammed" worship experiences. But you needn't enter the building to find a quiet spot for reflection and meditation. Just east of the meetinghouse is Friends Meditational Woods, which is open to the public. The grove has shade trees, a small waterfall, and plenty of options for seating.

Fittingly, the tranquil spot is home to a Peace Pole, which reads "May Peace Prevail on Earth" in several languages. Masahisa Goi, a Japanese poet and philosopher, conceived the Peace Pole Project in 1955 as a response to the bombings of Hiroshima and Nagasaki. Now the project is managed by the World Peace Prayer Society, and there are more than two hundred thousand Peace Poles worldwide, in almost every country on the planet. Each community designs its own Peace Pole, often using local materials, but all Peace Poles bear the "May Peace Prevail on Earth" message in the local language and in multiple translations.

Indy actually has several Peace Poles planted at churches, universities, and community gardens. Downtown Indy, Inc.,

---

Other tranquil spots for quiet reflection include the small meditation garden at Congregation Beth-El Zedeck and the Rivoli Park Labyrinth on Kealing Avenue. The latter is designed for meditative walks and is lovingly maintained by neighborhood volunteers.

A Peace Pole in the Friends Meditational Woods reads "May Peace Prevail on Earth" in English and several other languages. The quiet spot is just east of the Indianapolis First Friends meetinghouse.

installed one in its Pathways to Peace Garden, a pocket park at Indiana and Senate avenues. But, more so than the other locations, the Friends Meditational Woods is about finding inner peace, too.

FRIENDS MEDITATIONAL WOODS

WHAT A peaceful place for reflection and meditation

WHERE Indianapolis First Friends, 3030 Kessler Blvd. E. Dr.

COST Free

PRO TIP Indianapolis First Friends holds unprogrammed worship services in the Meditational Woods on many summer mornings.

25 A PROFILE IN COURAGE

How did one lone woman bring down the statewide Ku Klux Klan?

In the early 1920s, D. C. Stephenson ruled the state of Indiana from his home in Indy's Irvington neighborhood. As grand dragon of the state Ku Klux Klan, he used his money and influence to handpick government officials—even mayors and governors—who would follow his orders. He could do anything he pleased.

But then Stephenson noticed a young woman named Madge Oberholtzer, a government employee who lived nearby. She rejected his repeated advances, so he cooked up a new plan. One night in March 1925, he sent one of his bodyguards to "ask" for Oberholtzer's help with some emergency secretarial work. The messenger didn't even give her time to grab her hat. When she arrived at Stephenson's home she was drugged; later Stephenson loaded her into a private car on a train bound for Chicago and assaulted her for hours. They were at a hotel the next day when Oberholtzer begged for money to buy a hat at the drugstore. Despite being escorted by one of Stephenson's goons, she managed to buy several tablets of mercury bichloride, not enough to kill herself but enough to make herself so sick that surely Stephenson would take her home. Eventually he did, but Oberholtzer would die a month later from an infection in one of the wounds Stephenson had inflicted. As she lay dying, she bravely gave a statement about what had happened—one

---

Irvington Ghost Tours also discuss H. H. Holmes, "America's first serial killer" and the subject of the bestseller *Devil in the White City*. Holmes stayed in Irvington briefly in 1894 and committed at least one murder here.

Madge Oberholtzer died at the hands of D. C. Stephenson, the grand dragon of the Indiana Ku Klux Klan. But her dying declaration was airtight, and it put Stephenson in prison for murder—the beginning of the end for the Klan's hold on Indiana politics. Photo courtesy Indiana State Library.

IRVINGTON GHOST TOURS

WHAT A glimpse into Indy's ghostly past

WHERE 6 S. Johnson Ave.

COST $20 (cash only)

PRO TIP Tours are offered in October to coincide with Irvington's annual Halloween festival—easily one of the best seasonal events in Central Indiana. Don't miss it.

so clear, detailed, and candid that it is used as a model in law schools to this day. It was enough to put Stephenson in prison for murder, and it set in motion a series of events that forever destroyed the Klan's hold on Indiana politics.

You can thank Madge for her courage—in your mind, at least—during a walk with Indiana Ghost Tours. Both her home and Stephenson's are on the regular itinerary.

26 THE BOATLOAD OF KNOWLEDGE

Why does an Indy mural tell the story of tiny New Harmony, Indiana?

Kyle Ragsdale is one of the city's most prominent artists, so why would the Arts Council of Indianapolis commission him to paint a mural in a low-visibility location underneath a bridge? For one thing, the 128-foot wall was probably the only space large enough to accommodate Ragsdale's grand vision for the mural, called *Hoosier Hospitality on the Boatload of Knowledge*.

To understand the mural, you first need to know the history of a tiny town called New Harmony. The community in southwest Indiana was founded in 1814 by George Rapp, a German Lutheran minister who believed God wanted him to establish a utopia in the wilderness. That plan fizzled, and ten years later the settlers sold the entire settlement outright to Scottish industrialist Robert Owen. His utopian vision for New Harmony involved social equality, free education, and an emphasis on science and technology. So, in 1826, a group of scientists and other settlers traveled to New Harmony from Pittsburgh on a ninety-two-foot keelboat nicknamed "The Boatload of Knowledge." Owen's utopia was also a failure, but Ragsdale was inspired by the values of the doomed community. The passengers on his keelboat come from many different

---

The best-known mural from the "46 for XLVI" project is *My Affair with Kurt Vonnegut*. The sky-high portrait of the beloved Indiana author, by Pamela Bliss, graces the 300 block of Mass Ave.

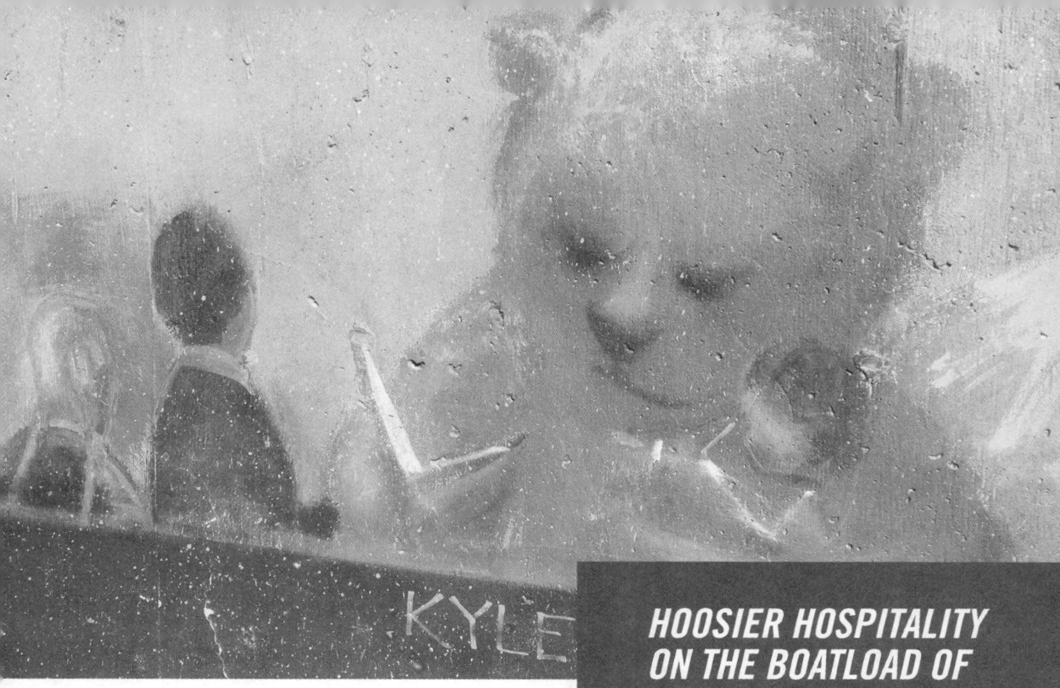

Located along the Canal Walk, the Hoosier Hospitality on the Boatload of Knowledge *mural tells a fascinating story from Indiana history. Artist Kyle Ragsdale's whimsical reimagining depicts a vibrant, diverse community of pioneer settlers with a shared utopian vision.*

HOOSIER HOSPITALITY ON THE BOATLOAD OF KNOWLEDGE

WHAT A historic mural with a modern twist

WHERE Canal Walk at Michigan Street

COST Free

PRO TIP To see more of Ragsdale's work, check out his studio at the Harrison Center for the Arts.

backgrounds, however, suggesting a more contemporary vision of harmony.

The Arts Council of Indianapolis commissioned the mural as part of "46 for XLVI," a public art project designed to spruce up the city before it hosted the Super Bowl in 2012. The project also included several other large murals along the Canal Walk, including *Love Letter Indiana* and *Quetzalcoatl Returns to Look in the Mirror* at West Street, *Return to Innocence* and *Morning Magnolias* at Ohio Street, *Morphos* and *Waterflow* at New York Street, and *White River Canal Aquaculture Preservation Aquarium* at Michigan Street.

27 FOOD FOR THOUGHT

Where in Indy can you learn to butcher whole hogs?

Goose the Market is a wonderland of specialty foods, but behind its success is the meaty magic of Smoking Goose. From its out-of-the-way location on Dorman Street, the Smoking Goose Meatery supplies cured and smoked meats, sausages, salumi, and larder meats to restaurants all across the Midwest.

In addition, the meatery's skilled butchers serve as teachers in the Smoking Goose Meat School. You can learn to break down whole hogs using traditional techniques, make sausages and pâté, or create salumi from scratch. You'll get your own Smoking Goose hat, as well as a behind-the-scenes tour, a private tasting, and lots of meaty goodies to take home.

The Smoking Goose Meatery also lets you become a butcher without quitting your day job. Simply join the Meat Minutemen program, no experience required. You'll be called in to help with big jobs, such as linking sausages, trussing hams, or tying salumi, and your payment will be—you guessed it—piles of meat.

SMOKING GOOSE MEAT SCHOOL

WHAT Butchering 101

WHERE 407 Dorman St.

COST $120–$150

NOTEWORTHY Smoking Goose has teamed up with Just Pop In to create a specialty popcorn flavor, a blend of caramel popcorn, cheddar popcorn, and candied bacon.

At the Smoking Goose Meat School, skilled butchers teach classes on butchering whole hogs and making sausages, pâté, and salumi. Classes also include private tastings and behind-the-scenes tours of the Smoking Goose Meatery. Photos courtesy Smoking Goose.

The Smoking Goose Meatery holds a meat sale once per month, offering wholesale pricing on a limited supply of smoked meats, sausages, salumi, and more.

28 OUR BIG FAT GREEK FRIEZE

Where in Indy can you see a rare replica of an Elgin Marble?

A purpose-built gallery at the British Museum in London displays the Elgin Marbles, the beautiful sculptures that once graced the Parthenon in Athens. But you don't have to cross the Atlantic to see one. Herron High School has a rare plaster replica of one of the Parthenon friezes, one of only a handful that survive worldwide.

The Elgin Marbles were sculpted around 435 BCE, and the Herron replica dates from about 1924. It was cast directly from the ancient marble frieze, but the practice was soon discontinued because of concerns about potential damage to the original friezes. Similar replicas—the few that exist—are generally held at museums, such as the Ashmolean Museum at the University of Oxford. The Herron frieze was installed in the Herron Main Building soon after it opened in 1928, and it may have been a gift from the Greek government to celebrate the growing school.

The frieze is more than five feet wide, and it is a replica of North Frieze Block XLVII. It most likely depicts the procession of the Panathenaic festival honoring the goddess Athena.

The real Elgin Marbles are mired in controversy. Greece has argued fiercely for their return from England, claiming that Thomas Bruce, the Seventh Earl of Elgin, took the sculptures in the early 1800s without permission. The British Museum has staunchly refused.

Herron High School owns a rare plaster replica of an Elgin Marble, one of the friezes that once graced the Parthenon in Athens. The replica was cast directly from the marble original circa 1924, and very few of its kind survive.

REPLICA OF ELGIN MARBLE

WHAT A rare plaster copy of a priceless Parthenon frieze

WHERE Herron High School, 110 E. Sixteenth St.

COST Free

PRO TIP School security is tight these days, so call ahead for an appointment.

These particular horsemen are still getting ready, however, and haven't yet joined the parade.

When the Herron School of Art and Design moved to the IUPUI campus in 2005, the frieze was left behind. For nearly a decade it was exposed to high humidity, freezing temperatures, and moisture from a leaking roof; other large plaster friezes simply crumbled. But Herron High School eventually claimed the campus, and in 2013 the frieze was carefully—very, very carefully—removed and stabilized. It was installed at the school's Russell Hall about a year later, after a brief stint at the City Gallery at the Harrison Center for the Arts.

29 THE TITANS OF INDUSTRY

Where can you find a giant pink elephant holding a martini?

Between 1963 and 1974, the International Fiberglass company produced thousands of twenty-foot human statues, such as lumberjacks, cowboys, astronauts, Vikings, and Mr. Bendo muffler men. Few of these statues survive—some were decapitated in high winds—but Indy does have an example of its own. One of the Mr. Bendo muffler men lives at Ralph's Muffler & Brake Service on Sixteenth Street. His muffler is gone, unfortunately, but he still stands tall in his beard and red work shirt.

Mr. Bendo is just one of Indy's giant advertising icons. Fortville has a giant pink elephant produced by Wisconsin-based DWO Fiberglass. The elephant wears glasses and swills a martini, and for decades he lived outside a liquor store. But the store recently closed, and the elephant is in search of a new home. He has become a local icon over the years, so no doubt he'll stay somewhere in Fortville.

Way back in the 1970s, the elephant lived at Cohron's Manufactured Homes on Pendleton Pike. And it had a friend, a giant cow, which still lives there. The cow's origin is uncertain, but it may have come from the local Choc-Ola factory. The company originally planned to sell the cow, but "it has since become a landmark for the community, not to mention an easy way for people to find our sales location," says Jacob Cohron. The company founders, who grew up on a farm in rural Kentucky, even incorporated the cow into the logo.

The giant cow at Cohron's Manufactured Homes is usually black and white, but it sometimes gets a festive paint job to support local sports teams.

GIANT ADVERTISING ICONS

WHAT Larger-than-life fiberglass statues

WHERE Mr. Bendo: 1250 W. Sixteenth St.; giant pink elephant: Fortville; giant cow: 9623 Pendleton Pike

COST Free

PRO TIP Farther afield, the Indiana Basketball Hall of Fame in New Castle has a giant tennis shoe, and a farm market in Bruceville has a giant peach (James not included).

We Hoosiers love our giant fiberglass animals. This giant cow on Pendleton Pike has been the symbol of Cohron's Manufactured Homes for half a century. Photo courtesy Cohron's Manufactured Homes.

Indy's other giants include the Galyan's bear sculpture at Eagle Creek Park, dinosaurs outside The Children's Museum of Indianapolis, green trowels at several Habig Garden Shop locations, and a steaming pot of soup at Zesco Restaurant Supply.

30 THE LONG ARM OF THE LAW

Where can you find a copy of John Dillinger's death mask?

The Indiana State Police Museum doesn't appear to get much foot traffic. On the morning I visited, I had the museum completely to myself, and the staff even seemed somewhat surprised to have a visitor. But that's a shame, because this small museum has some exhibits worth exploring.

The highlight of the museum is the collection of police cars, including a 1938 Chevrolet manufactured just five years after the department was founded. A small display case in the next room contains objects related to bank robber John Dillinger, including a copy of his death mask and a replica of the wooden gun he once used to escape from prison. Other artifacts on display include police uniforms and weaponry, traffic signals, an early polygraph machine, a bulky antique Drunkometer, and several antique slot machines seized by the police.

INDIANA STATE POLICE MUSEUM

WHAT A closer look at police procedure

WHERE 8660 E. Twenty-First St.

COST Free

PRO TIP Consider combining your visit here with a trip to the Koorsen Fire Museum just a few miles away.

Exhibits throughout the museum describe the many different facets of police work, such as the bomb squad, the K-9 unit, the scuba team, and the forensics laboratory. Guided tours are available on request, but note that the museum's only weekend hours are from noon to 4 p.m. on the third Saturday of each month.

Vintage police cars are the star attraction at the Indiana State Police Museum, which also displays early polygraph machines, antique breathalyzers, and several artifacts related to bank robber John Dillinger.

At the Indiana State Police Museum, a wall of photos near the front door memorializes officers killed in the line of duty.

31 A RELIC OF DINOSAUR DIGESTION

What can we learn from fossilized dinosaur poop?

Some days, paleontologists have a seemingly glamorous job, digging for fossils and assembling dinosaur skeletons, such as the newly discovered *Dracorex hogwartsia*, the "dragon king of Hogwarts." Other days, paleontologists do less glamorous work—for example, studying coprolites (a.k.a. fossilized animal dung).

The Children's Museum of Indianapolis has eleven coprolites in its collection (along with a *Dracorex hogwartsia* skeleton). The oldest and largest of the coprolites is from the Jurassic period, roughly 150 million years ago, and was found in Colorado. The others are more recent—about 30 million years old. They were formed the same way all fossils are formed: organic material was buried in the ground, and over time seeping water replaced the organic material with minerals.

But what can scientists actually learn from coprolite? Quite a lot, says William Ripley, the museum's curator of natural science. "At the minimum you can learn, based on what you can observe in the sample, whether the animal leaving it behind ate meat or plant materials," Ripley says. "That can then lead to learning what *types* of animal or plant species roamed particular areas during certain time frames." Scientists can also learn about the

---

Other unusual artifacts at The Children's Museum of Indianapolis include Amelia Earhart's aviator goggles, a Golden Ticket from the 1971 movie *Willy Wonka and the Chocolate Factory*, and a coffin shaped like a tennis shoe.

Each coprolite—a piece of fossilized animal dung—has a story to tell. Scientists can learn what an animal ate and how it digested its food, as well as what plants and animals lived in the area at a particular time. Photo courtesy The Children's Museum of Indianapolis.

COPROLITES

WHAT Fossilized animal dung

WHERE The Children's Museum of Indianapolis, 3000 N. Meridian St.

COST $23.50 for adults, $19 for kids

PRO TIP To learn more about coprolites, have a chat with the paleontologists in the Paleo Lab, part of the museum's Dinosphere exhibit.

animal's digestive system, such as whether the animal chewed its food or swallowed chunks whole. And, as technology improves, scientists are finding even more ways to extract data from ancient coprolites. Who knew old poop could be so informative?

32 THE EVIDENCE IN THE EARTHWORKS

What is the most important archaeological site in Central Indiana?

In the early years of pioneer settlement, Indiana farmers routinely plowed over the raised earthworks (i.e., dirt mounds) left behind by prehistoric tribes, gradually wearing them away to nothing. When Eli Lilly described the earthworks near Strawtown in his 1937 book, *Prehistoric Antiquities of Indiana*, he lamented that the former Native American settlement, like many others, was "all but obliterated" and "had almost disappeared." Today, however, archaeologists are working to restore the lost knowledge of this important prehistoric site.

The settlement that Lilly described is now within Strawtown Koteewi Park, an eight-hundred-acre swath of prairie, wetlands, and woodlands in Hamilton County. The village was a circular earthwork about three hundred feet in diameter, surrounded by a wooden palisade and a ditch about six feet deep. "That an extensive village once occupied practically the whole of the high ground is proved by the frequent finding of both human and animal bones, projectile points, pieces of flint, and many potsherds," Lilly wrote. Archaeologists now believe that the village was inhabited by Native Americans from the Oliver Phase, a prehistoric cultural group that lived along the White River from 1200 to 1450 AD.

At the Taylor Center of Natural History, you can examine many artifacts from the Oliver Phase, such as pottery, arrowheads,

---

Koteewi is the Miami word for "prairie" and is pronounced ko-TAY-wee.

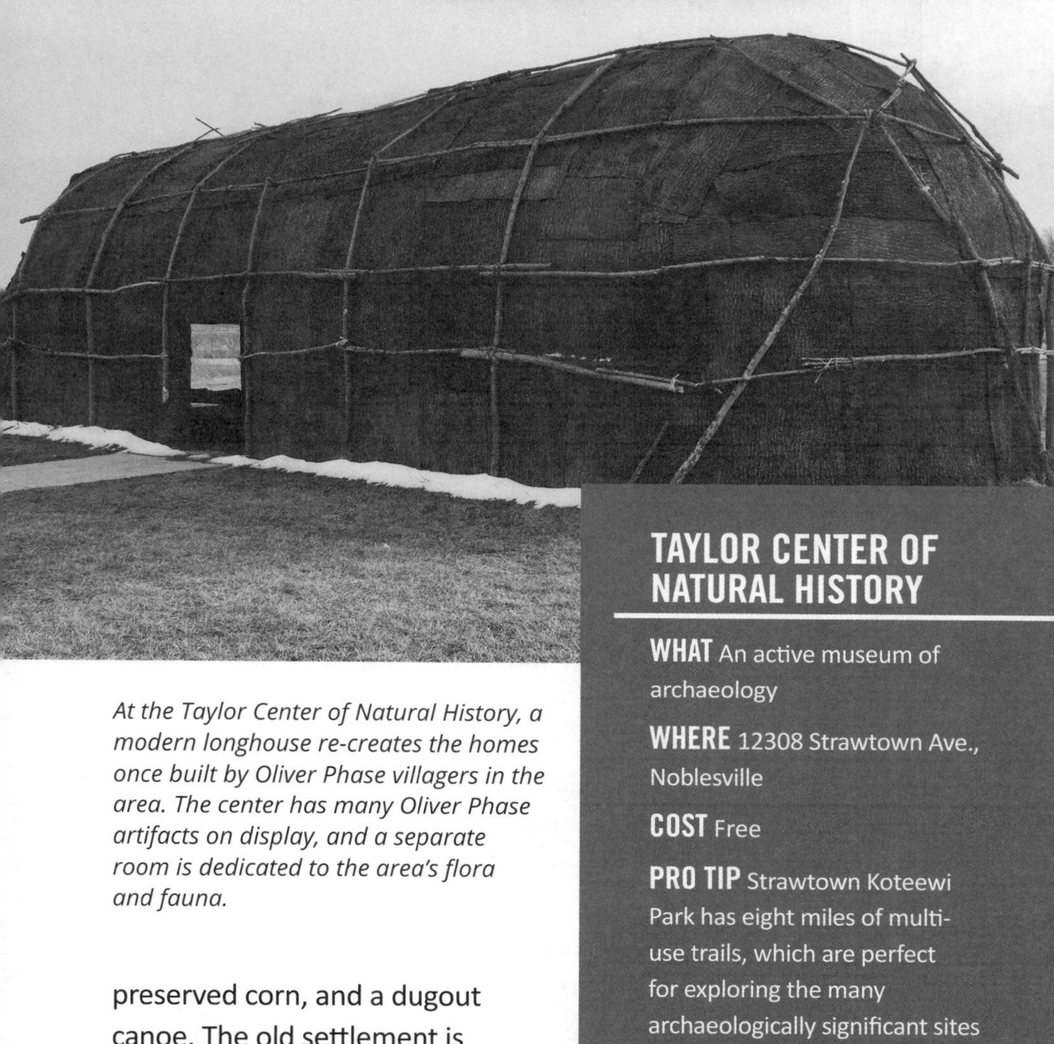

At the Taylor Center of Natural History, a modern longhouse re-creates the homes once built by Oliver Phase villagers in the area. The center has many Oliver Phase artifacts on display, and a separate room is dedicated to the area's flora and fauna.

TAYLOR CENTER OF NATURAL HISTORY

WHAT An active museum of archaeology

WHERE 12308 Strawtown Ave., Noblesville

COST Free

PRO TIP Strawtown Koteewi Park has eight miles of multi-use trails, which are perfect for exploring the many archaeologically significant sites in the area.

preserved corn, and a dugout canoe. The old settlement is located just steps away, and the surrounding ditch is still faintly visible. Yes, it has almost disappeared—but not entirely. The site still has many things to teach us about Hoosier history. The archaeologists here are passionate about their subject and generous with their time, so feel free to ask plenty of questions.

33 AN OFFICE FIT FOR A PHARAOH

Why does Indy have a trio of pyramids?

Architectural innovation isn't something we usually associate with suburban office parks. But the Pyramids are an exception. Originally the headquarters for the College Life Insurance Company, the buildings were designed by one of the world's top architects, Kevin Roche.

A winner of the prestigious Pritzker Architecture Prize, Roche designed thirty-eight corporate headquarters for companies such as John Deere, General Foods, Leo Burnett, J. P. Morgan, Union Carbide, and Merck. He spent a decade working with Eero Saarinen, the creator of the Gateway Arch in St. Louis, and he completed many of Saarinen's projects after the architect's sudden death in 1961. He also developed the master architectural plan for the Metropolitan Museum of Art and designed several of its expansions, including the famous glass pavilion that houses the Temple of Dendur.

Roche designed the Pyramids with reinforced concrete cores that could support the entire building, without any need for internal structural supports. So the Pyramids allowed for open-plan workspaces long before that layout was the norm. Each

---

Architect Kevin Roche had a close connection with Cummins chairman J. Irwin Miller. Roche assisted Eero Saarinen with Miller's home in Columbus, Indiana. He later designed several Cummins buildings, including its corporate headquarters, as well as Miller's vacation home in Florida.

The Pyramids may inhabit a suburban office park, but they were designed by one of the world's top architects, Kevin Roche. A former protégé of Eero Saarinen and a winner of the prestigious Pritzker Architecture Prize, Roche designed thirty-eight corporate headquarters and several wings at the Metropolitan Museum of Art.

THE PYRAMIDS

WHAT Indy's most recognizable architectural silhouettes

WHERE 3500 DePauw Blvd.

COST Free

PRO TIP The café in Pyramid 3 is a good option if you're looking for an excuse to peek inside the buildings.

eleven-story building has two glass curtain walls, with reflective glass that was inspired by a pair of Roche's sunglasses.

The first three Pyramids were completed in 1972. College Life Insurance Company planned to add six more buildings over time, in a three by three grid, to accommodate future growth. But the company moved out of state after a merger, and since then the Pyramids have been leased to other tenants. Current tenants include AT&T, the Indiana Institute of Technology, and many attorneys, medical practices, financial advisors, and nonprofit organizations.

34 THE WINDS OF WAR

Which downtown memorial contains a secret museum?

The Indiana War Memorial, which honors fallen soldiers from the Hoosier state, stands tall on its downtown plaza. The striking neoclassical building is clad in Indiana limestone, and its sculptures depict virtues such as courage, victory, and patriotism. The memorial is a fitting tribute all on its own, so it may not have occurred to you to actually go *inside*.

Start your tour in the basement, where a surprisingly large museum details Hoosier military involvement in every campaign from the Battle of Tippecanoe to the present. On display are weapons, uniforms, battle flags, and other artifacts, including an actual AH-1 Cobra attack helicopter. The museum relies heavily on dioramas peopled with mannequins, so it isn't particularly interactive. But every now and then there's a surprise, such as a re-created World War I trench that you can walk through.

On the first floor you'll find several exhibition galleries. One tells the story of the cruiser USS *Indianapolis*, which was sunk in 1945. (For a single ship, it was the highest death toll in the history of the US Navy.) When you see the large auditorium on this floor, you may start to wonder whether the Indiana War Memorial is actually the TARDIS in a limestone disguise.

On the top floor is the Shrine Room, a beautiful and peaceful space designed to honor Indiana soldiers who gave their lives. It is decorated with materials from all over the world to symbolize

---

The Canal Walk, stretching from White River State Park to Eleventh Street, is home to both the national USS *Indianapolis* memorial and the Congressional Medal of Honor Memorial.

An AH-1 Cobra attack helicopter fills an entire room at the Indiana War Memorial Museum. The hidden museum inside the Indiana War Memorial tells more than two hundred years of Hoosier war stories.

INDIANA WAR MEMORIAL MUSEUM

WHAT An under-the-radar military museum

WHERE 431 N. Meridian St.

COST Free

NOTEWORTHY The museum's collection contains many artifacts from the former Colonel Eli Lilly Civil War Museum, which was located inside the Soldiers and Sailors Monument prior to its closure.

unity, but with an American twist—red marble columns; a white, star-shaped crystal light fixture; and blue-tinted windows and lights. The white frieze wrapped around the room tells the story of war: preparation for war, the war itself, and victory. At the center of the room, a large US flag hangs suspended above an "Altar of Consecration" to the beloved Stars and Stripes.

35 A STATUE THAT SHOWS A LITTLE LEG

What happened to the rest of this Georgia Street sculpture?

After completing its duties related to Super Bowl XLVI, the 2012 Indianapolis Super Bowl Host Committee presented the city with a gift—a bronze sculpture at the intersection of Georgia and Meridian streets. Unveiled that March, the sculpture depicts Hoosier basketball legend John Wooden, one of the winningest coaches of all time. It should have been a slam dunk, but instead horrified locals cried foul.

The base of the sculpture, which is called *Wooden's Legacy*, is inscribed with words such as loyalty, self-control, cooperation, and confidence—all part of Wooden's legendary Pyramid of Success. Wooden himself is depicted in a familiar position, kneeling among his players and grasping a rolled-up playbook. Except, well, he isn't actually kneeling among players. He's kneeling among five pairs of disembodied legs, all chopped off mid-thigh. Lou Harry, the arts and entertainment reporter for the *Indianapolis Business Journal*, wrote that "it looks like Wooden is holding forth in a Nordstrom window display warehouse, or presiding over an early stop on the leg lamp assembly line." And Sam Stall, who writes the Hoosierist column for *Indianapolis Monthly*, wondered why anyone would "show one of Indiana's most beloved sports icons crouching among a bunch of

---

As coach of the UCLA Bruins, John Wooden racked up four perfect seasons, twenty conference championships, thirty-eight NCAA tournament appearances, and ten national championships—seven of them consecutive.

Unveiled in 2012, the bronze Wooden's Legacy *sculpture depicts Hoosier basketball legend John Wooden surrounded by his players—well, portions of them, at least. Wooden died in 2010 at the age of ninety-nine. Photo courtesy Downtown Indy, Inc.*

WOODEN'S LEGACY

WHAT A much-maligned tribute to a basketball legend

WHERE 2 W. Georgia St.

COST Free

NOTEWORTHY John Wooden was the first man to be inducted into the Basketball Hall of Fame twice, as both a player and a coach.

mannequin legs like a lunatic hiding in a department store."

To be fair, the legs do tell part of the story. The shoes and socks are historically accurate for four key phases of Wooden's career—his time as an all-star player at Martinsville High School and Purdue University, his early coaching years at Indiana State University, and his first and last NCAA championship wins with the UCLA Bruins. The fifth player is meant to represent the future of basketball. The sculpture survived a head-on collision with a car in 2015, so for the foreseeable future we're stuck with *Wooden's Legacy*.

36 A PASSAGE TO INDIA

Where can you find the full spectrum of Hindu traditions in one place?

When the Hindu Temple of Central Indiana opened in 2006, it was the first of its kind in the state, and it was a welcome addition for thousands of local Hindu families. But at first the congregation couldn't afford the architectural embellishments so common to temples in India. Devotees worshipped in a temporary space, and the spartan building rarely attracted much attention.

In 2015, however, the temple completed an impressive $10 million expansion. The new worship hall has seventeen beautiful shrines, some modeled on famous temples in India. And four elaborately carved towers have been added to the roof, one above the entrance and three directly above the main shrines in the worship hall. Nearly five thousand people attended the final day of the grand opening ceremonies, and a thousand or more visit the temple on important Hindu holidays.

In India, the different sects of Hinduism have their own temples. But that model isn't financially viable in Indiana, where less than 1 percent of the population identifies as Hindu. So the Hindu Temple of Central Indiana is unique, in that it brings together many different Hindu traditions under one roof.

The Hindu Temple of Central Indiana, which serves many different Hindu sects, is guided by a quote from the Rigveda: "The Truth is One, though the wise may call it by many names."

The Hindu Temple of Central Indiana once resembled a plain warehouse. But a $10 million expansion in 2015 transformed the building, adding four towers, a new worship hall, and countless architectural embellishments.

HINDU TEMPLE OF CENTRAL INDIANA

WHAT A pilgrimage across India, all in one place

WHERE 3350 N. German Church Rd.

COST Free

PRO TIP To schedule a tour, email tours@htci.org at least two weeks in advance.

Visitors are welcome at the temple, and free guided tours are available by appointment. Guides discuss the basics of Hinduism and explain "how the spaces and symbols of the temple help the spiritual journey," according to the website. Dress in clean, modest clothing and come prepared to sit on the floor. And choose your socks wisely, as you'll be asked to leave your shoes in the lobby.

37 A "COUNT THE COUNTIES" SCAVENGER HUNT

Why is Garfield trapped in a canning jar at White River State Park?

On the grounds of the Indiana State Museum, an unusual scavenger hunt can quickly become a crash course in Indiana history and culture. An intriguing outdoor feature called the 92 County Walk features sculptures representing every Indiana county, from Adams to Whitely. Some are embedded in the museum walls, and others are built into the sidewalks and stairs. And it's a fun challenge to track them all down.

The sculptures often have a refreshing sense of humor. Delaware County is the birthplace of both Ball canning jars and the Garfield comic strip, and its sculpture depicts a stack of nine jars, one of which has Garfield trapped inside. Whitely County is a farming community that also produces world-renowned bassoons, so its sculpture is a cross between a wind instrument and a cornstalk. And, in the Grant County sculpture, native James Dean pokes his head out of a bag of locally grown popcorn.

Start your scavenger hunt with these thirty surprises:

- Airplane on a basketball court
- Apple tree made of arrows
- Blue glass flame
- Boat inside a covered bridge
- Egg-shaped globe
- Face in a lightbulb
- Face of Abraham Lincoln
- Hood ornament
- Hot dog on a fork
- Hula-hooper
- Labyrinth
- Lighthouse
- Map of Indy's Mile Square
- Open book
- Open car door
- Paddleboat
- Pumpkin/pig
- Round barn
- Sand dunes
- Set of drawers
- Spaceship
- Tecumseh
- Three marching turtles
- Tiny Mickey Mouse
- Tiny tree
- Toboggan
- Trapeze artist
- Trumpet
- Turkey mosaic
- Typewriter

92 COUNTY WALK

WHAT A treasure hunt with a Hoosier twist

WHERE Indiana State Museum (exterior), 650 W. Washington St.

COST Free

PRO TIP For more information about each sculpture, pick up a copy of the museum's book *The Art of the 92 County Walk.*

The 92 County Walk features sculptures that represent every Indiana county. This Whitely County sculpture playfully celebrates the area's farming heritage and its world-renowned bassoon industry. Photo courtesy Indiana State Museum and Historic Sites.

Many of the county sculptures are carved in limestone, but the series also incorporates materials such as glass, bronze, steel, and ceramic tiles.

38 AN ADVENTURE IN WONDERLAND

Which Indy venue offers the weirdest slate of entertainment?

Don't be late for your very important date at the White Rabbit Cabaret. The performance lineup at this Fountain Square venue is both weird and wonderful, just like the Wonderland inhabited by the White Rabbit, the Mad Hatter, the Queen of Hearts, and the Cheshire Cat.

You might see the spoofy Let's Make a Date Gameshow, a crowd favorite that has been running for more than five years. Lloyd and Harvey's Wowie Zowie Show features kooky variety acts, and the Burlesque Bingo Bango Show mixes old-school bingo with bizarre prizes and irreverent hijinks. And the ongoing Upland Free Time Movie Series intentionally screens films of dubious quality, such as *Space Jam*, *What About Bob*, and *Road House*, complete with door prizes and themed drink specials.

White Rabbit is also ground zero for Indy's burgeoning burlesque scene. Performances by troupes such as the Rocket Doll Revue are a body-positive delight—hilarious rather than salacious—and are perfect for a raucous girls' night out. Touring burlesque troupes often land here, too.

Don't be fooled by White Rabbit's regular "An Evening with the Authors" events. The books are fake. The authors are fake. Only the comedy is real.

The Muncie Brothers (Dorgan and Milroy Muncie) and Alabaster Betty emcee one of White Rabbit Cabaret's most popular events, the Burlesque Bingo Bango Show. Imagine the bingo you know and love, but with prizes such as horse masks and portable camping toilets. Photo courtesy gregthemayor.

WHITE RABBIT CABARET

WHAT A weird and wonderful entertainment venue

WHERE 1116 Prospect St.

COST Varies

PRO TIP Start your night down the street at New Day Craft. The tasting room pours out tasting flights of New Day's delicious hard ciders and meads (honey-based wines).

White Rabbit also has more traditional offerings, such as trivia nights, dance parties, live music, and both improv and stand-up comedy. You must be twenty-one with a valid ID to enter; tickets are sometimes available in advance online, but otherwise come prepared to pay cash at the door.

39 A TRAGEDY ON THE UNDERGROUND RAILROAD

Do escaped slaves still haunt this southside mansion?

The Hannah House is often called the most haunted building in Indiana. Over the years, its owners have reported the sounds of footsteps, moaning, and breaking glass, plus unusual smells and cold spots. Doors open and close of their own accord, pictures fall off walls for no reason, spoons go flying through the air, and stereos shut off by themselves. And more than one resident has reported seeing—even talking to—a man with muttonchop sideburns, who then vanishes.

The brick home was built in 1858 by Alexander Hannah, a businessman, philanthropist, and state legislator. Hannah was also a staunch abolitionist, and legend states that his home—then secluded on a large wooded estate—was a stop on the Underground Railroad. Men, women, and children who had escaped from slavery were hidden in the basement, in a secret room that locked from the outside. One night, the story goes, someone in the room accidentally knocked over an oil lamp. The room was engulfed in smoke and flames, and several people died before Hannah could unlock the door. The dead were then hastily buried under the basement's dirt floor, and ghost hunters claim that their spirits still haunt the aging mansion.

Indiana's oldest bar, the Slippery Noodle, was also part of the Underground Railroad network. It reportedly has several ghosts of its own.

The Hannah House was built in 1858 and was, according to legend, an important station on the Underground Railroad. Many say it is haunted by the ghosts of escaped slaves who died here in an accidental fire.

THE HANNAH HOUSE

WHAT A haunted relic of the Underground Railroad

WHERE 3801 Madison Ave.

COST Not open to the public

PRO TIP Alexander Hannah and his wife, Elizabeth, are buried in Crown Hill Cemetery—always worth a visit for the outstanding public tours.

The house has changed hands many times since then, at various times serving as an antique store and event venue. For several decades it simply sat vacant. In the 1980s, the Indianapolis Junior Chamber of Commerce capitalized on its reputation by staging haunted houses there each October. At the moment the house is closed to the public, but you can still spot it from the road.

40 THE DREAM MACHINE

Where can you find a musical sandbox and a twisted house?

The Indianapolis Art Center is known for its arts education programs, from two-hour "make it, take it" pop-up classes to semester-long courses in painting, ceramics, glassblowing, metalworking, and more. But the Art Center also offers a lesser-known arts experience, right in its own backyard: the ArtsPark. The ten-acre greenspace was designed by architect (and Indiana native) Michael Graves, and the grounds are dotted with more than two dozen interactive sculptures.

Some of the installations in this "gallery without walls" are temporary, so the ArtsPark experience is constantly changing. Other installations, such as the oddball *Twisted House* by woodworking artist John McNaughton, are permanent. Look for towering metal sculptures, a sandbox that plays music, a "dream machine" chair, an imploding cube, a brightly painted mural, and more.

Each May the ArtsPark hosts the Broad Ripple Art Fair, a juried

ArtsPark

WHAT An oasis of quirky outdoor art

WHERE Indianapolis Art Center, 820 E. Sixty-Seventh St.

COST Free

NOTEWORTHY Originally called the Indianapolis Art League, the Indianapolis Art Center was founded in 1934 as a project of the Works Progress Administration.

The official name of the "dream machine" is *Sometimes I Sits*. The steel sculpture was inspired by a poster that read "Sometimes I sits and thinks, and sometimes I just sits." And, yes, you can sit on it.

Designed by Michael Graves, the ArtsPark at the Indianapolis Art Center is an outdoor gallery for sculptural installations such as the blue tiled Crescendo *and a "dream machine." Photos courtesy Dion Hazelbaker.*

event featuring the work of more than two hundred artists and artisans. It is the Art Center's largest annual fundraiser and also features live music, local beers, and tons of food choices. It's a wonderful event, but don't make it your only visit to the ArtsPark. The park is perfect throughout the year for casual walks, quiet contemplation, and perhaps even artistic inspiration.

41 AN ART DECO DELIGHT

How did the discovery of King Tut's tomb influence Indy architecture?

For years after its construction, the Soldiers and Sailors Monument was the tallest building on Monument Circle—by law. A zoning ordinance forbade taller buildings so that the monument would never be overshadowed. In 1922, however, the ordinance was changed: a building still couldn't cast a shadow on the monument, but it *could* be taller than the monument if that condition was met.

A few years later, the Tower Realty Company announced plans for a new fourteen-story building on the Circle's southeast side. But how could such a tall building meet the "cast no shadow" rule? The architectural firm of Rubush and Hunter solved the problem using setback construction: starting at floor eleven, each floor was set back from the one below, in a pattern resembling an ancient ziggurat. It was the first building of its kind in the city.

Circle Tower was completed just eight years after the discovery of King Tut's tomb, and the architects—like everyone else at the time—were fascinated by all things Egyptian. Note the bronze Egyptian figures that decorate the two-story entrance on Market Street. Even more Art Deco motifs are inside, in the lobby. Elevator doors made of solid bronze gleam against the black marble walls, and even the mailbox is beautiful. Don't be afraid to go in and take a peek.

For more Art Deco architecture, check out the former Coca-Cola bottling plant on the 800 block of Mass Ave. Built in 1931, it was also designed by Rubush and Hunter.

CIRCLE TOWER

WHAT An Art Deco lobby gleaming with bronze

WHERE 55 Monument Circle

COST Free

PRO TIP Indiana Landmarks also offers tours of the City Market Catacombs and the historic Athenaeum building.

Hidden inside the Circle Tower building on Monument Circle is a beautiful Art Deco lobby. Decorated with black marble and bronze, it was inspired by the international craze for Egyptian imagery at that time.

For more context, visit Circle Tower as part of the free Monument Circle walking tour offered by Indiana Landmarks (indianalandmarks.org). The knowledgeable guides will point out all kinds of things you never noticed about Monument Circle. (Have you ever spotted the carved stone frog on the exterior of the Columbia Club? Can you guess why it's there?) Tours are offered at 10 a.m., Fridays and Saturdays, from May to October.

42 A STORIED TRADITION

Where in Indy can you tell your own tales?

Oral storytelling is one of humankind's oldest forms of entertainment, and it has always been an important part of our culture. The tradition our ancestors started around their campfires gave rise to the wandering bards of medieval Europe, the fairy tales we tell our children, and even modern TED Talks.

This ancient art is championed locally by Storytelling Arts of Indiana. The small organization coordinates more than a hundred events each year, from "storytelling concerts" to lying contests. Some of its "tellers" are national names, and others are historians seeking to resurrect forgotten stories. But absolutely anyone can become a teller at the Indy Story Slam. All you need is a true, first-person story that you can tell in five minutes or less, without using any props or notes. "There's a lot of energy because of the competition, but the audience is very supportive," says executive director Ellen Munds. The winner gets $50 and sometimes an invitation to speak at a more formal Storytelling Arts event. And if that sounds way too intimidating, you can still participate as a judge, time keeper, or score keeper, or simply listen.

Ultimately, the slam encourages audiences to tell their own stories—perhaps at the dinner table instead of on stage. "We want people to enjoy storytelling as an art form," Munds says. "But we also want people to realize that they all have stories to share, and that their stories are of value."

INDY STORY SLAM

WHAT An epic open-mic storytelling contest

WHERE IndyFringe Basile Theatre, 719 E. St. Clair St.

COST $10

PRO TIP The slam is held six times each year, monthly from September to November and again from February to April.

Through its Indy Story Slam events, Storytelling Arts of Indiana is breathing new life into an ancient artform. A Tale from the Decameron, *John William Waterhouse (1916). Image courtesy Wikimedia Commons.*

Many Storytelling Arts of Indiana performances take place at the Indiana History Center, in partnership with the Indiana Historical Society.

43 A SKYSCRAPER OF ICE

Where can you find the largest icicles in town?

Indiana weather may be frightful in the winter, but every cloud has a silver lining. When temperatures dip below freezing, members of the Veal family set to work creating their beloved seasonal attraction, the Ice Tree, a tower of ice that sometimes climbs eighty feet high.

The story of the Ice Tree begins in 1961. That winter, Vierl G. Veal decided to turn a hill on the family's property into an ice slide for his children. He left hoses on overnight to spray water on the hill, but strong winds instead blew the mist onto a nearby cluster of honeysuckle bushes. The family loved the impromptu sculpture, and a tradition was born.

Technically, the Ice Tree is no longer a tree. Each year the family builds a supporting structure of scrap lumber and twine, making "branches" out of fresh-cut brush from the fence rows. Water pumped from the nearby pond coats the structure in layer after layer of ice, and the family sprays the ice with colorful dye for an extra visual punch. The colder the winter, the bigger the tree—so now you have something to look forward to the next time the Polar Vortex blows into town.

For more frozen fun, try Carmel's newest annual event, the Festival of Ice. Activities include ice skating, a chili cook-off, and an ice-carving competition.

VEAL'S ICE TREE

WHAT A frozen monolith with a fun family history

WHERE 11333 Southeastern Ave.

COST Free

PRO TIP Your GPS may lead you astray. From I-74, take the Acton Road exit and head south. Turn left at the first road (Southeastern Avenue) and left again into the first drive after the sharp curve.

The Veal family has been constructing its annual Ice Tree since 1961, when a hose left on overnight turned some nearby honeysuckle bushes into a glittering work of art. The record height is about eighty feet. Photo courtesy Janet Veal-Drummond.

THE EVIDENCE IN THE EARTHWORKS (page 64)

A FITTING TRIBUTE TO FIRE-FIGHTING (page 6)

A ROMAN HOLLIDAY (page 172)

A TUTU OR TWO (page 115)

VEAL'S ICE TREE (page 87)

AN ARTSY WAY TO STOP TRAFFIC (page 198)

A HOME FOR GNOMES (page 176)

A CURIOUS COSTUME CONTEST (page 28)

A SHORT TRIP AROUND THE WORLD (page 156)

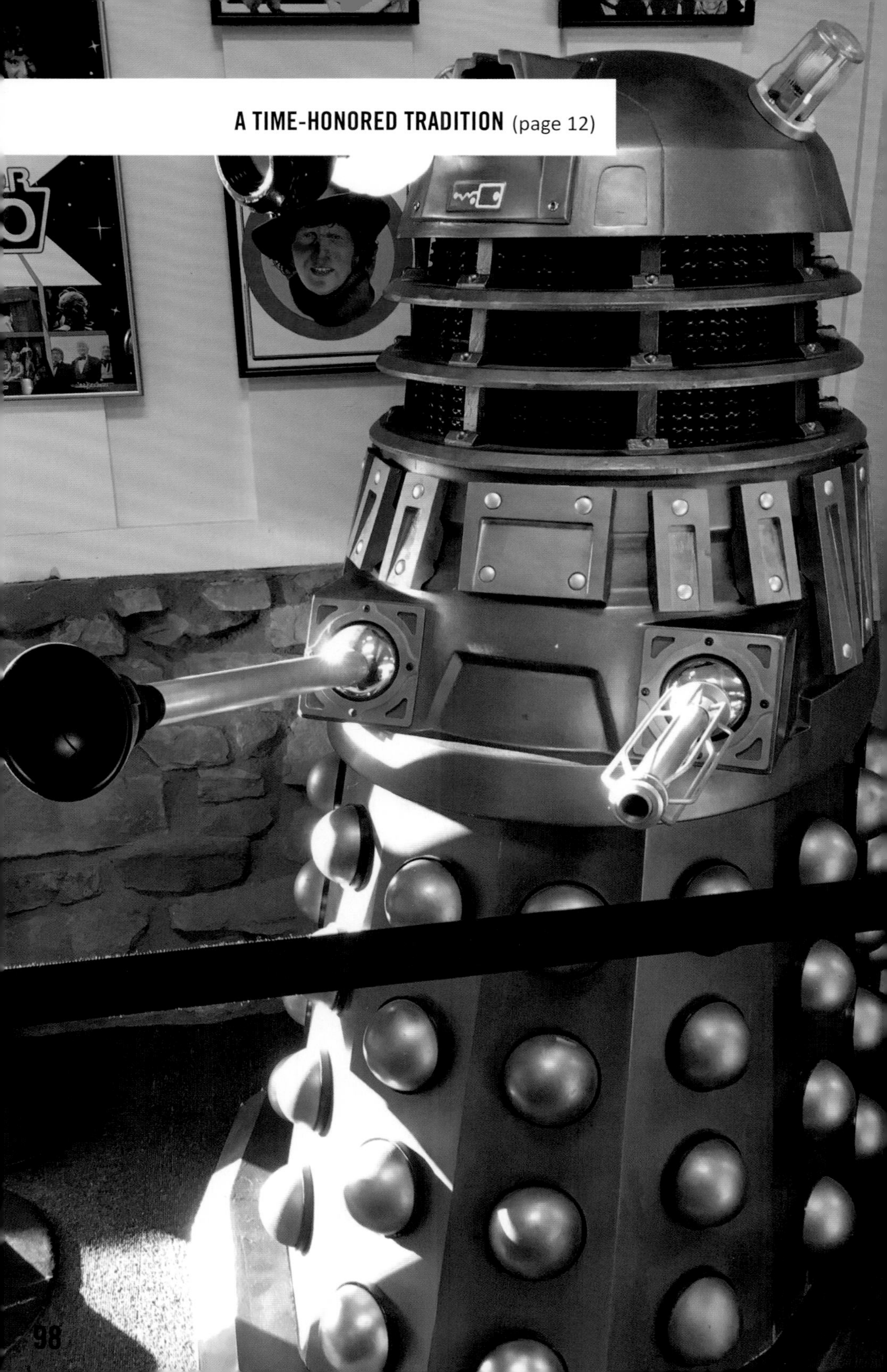

A TIME-HONORED TRADITION (page 12)

A WHIRLWIND VISIT (page 130)

THE BOATLOAD OF KNOWLEDGE (page 52)

THE TITANS OF INDUSTRY (page 58)

A STATUE THAT SHOWS A LITTLE LEG (page 70)

A GALLERY OF GRAFFITI (page 36)

THE CITY'S LARGEST COSTUME PARTY (page 152)

44 A PRESIDENTIAL PRANK

How did angry Hoosiers get even with Martin Van Buren?

Before the advent of railroads, pioneer settlements in Central Indiana were hugely dependent on US 40, the nation's first highway. Then called the National Road, the east-west route enabled Hoosiers to sell their products in larger markets—for much higher prices.

THE VAN BUREN ELM

WHAT A practical joke with a political purpose

WHERE Front lawn of the Friends Meetinghouse, 205 S. East St., Plainfield

COST Free

NOTEWORTHY The bribe the stagecoach driver received was a silk hat worth about $5.

Yet the road through Indiana was always in terrible shape, mired in mud and clogged with tree stumps, logs, and weeds. The ruts were so deep that travelers often tied themselves to their seats to keep from falling out. But in the late 1830s, during the presidency of Martin Van Buren, federal funding for the road dried up. Some Hoosiers never forgave him.

Skip to 1842, when Van Buren—now out of office but drumming up support for another run at the presidency—set out along the National Road by stagecoach. Plainfield residents were determined to show Van Buren how bad the road could be, so they bribed his stagecoach driver to give him a demonstration. The driver picked up speed coming down a hill, then intentionally drove over the roots of a large elm tree. The carriage overturned, and Van Buren was tossed out, straight into an enormous mud puddle.

News of the mishap ran in newspapers across the nation, and the tree became known as the Van Buren Elm. When it eventually died, Plainfield residents marked the spot with a commemorative plaque and planted another elm.

Former president Martin Van Buren was back on the campaign trail in 1842, trying to build support for another presidential bid. But a "mishap" in Plainfield that year put Van Buren in the papers for all the wrong reasons. Photo courtesy the Library of Congress.

Another tree with an unusual backstory is the "moon tree," a sycamore at the Indiana Statehouse. It grew from a seed that Apollo 14 astronauts had carried to the moon and back, just to see what would happen.

45 THE JOKE OF THE WEEK

Why is an insurance company known for its sense of humor?

Commuters in downtown Indianapolis get a weekly dose of humor from an unusual source—a corporate signboard. For more than sixty years, insurance company OneAmerica has decorated its signboards with puns so terrible that drivers can't help but laugh.

ONEAMERICA SIGNBOARDS

WHAT Signboards with a sense of humor

WHERE OneAmerica Tower, 1 American Square

COST Free

PRO TIP If you have a joke worth sharing, submit your idea at oneamerica.com/about-us/in-the-community/signboard. The company especially welcomes jokes related to upcoming holidays and local events, but nothing rude, political, or inspirational.

The tradition began in 1958, during the construction of a new headquarters for American United Life (now part of OneAmerica) along Fall Creek Parkway. The company erected a signboard apologizing to commuters for construction-related traffic delays. But the company president at the time thought humor might get more attention, and he was right. When the company moved downtown to its current home in 1982, public demand for the signboards heavily outweighed architects' concerns that the signboards would look out of place.

OneAmerica posts photos of the signboards each week on its Twitter feed (@oneamerica) so you can share the joke without facing the commute.

The puns are all intended on OneAmerica's downtown signboards. The insurance company has been giving commuters a weekly dose of humor since 1958. Photo courtesy OneAmerica.

The signboard sayings are often seasonal. In December, for example, the signs might say, "The best candy canes are in mint condition" or "Christmas trees really spruce things up." Sometimes the signs ask fundamental life questions, such as "Why is abbreviated such a long word?" But generally the signs just have fun with puns. Take, for example, these recent favorites:

"Geology rocks, but geography is where it's at."
"You can push the envelope, but it will remain stationery."
"I did not invent gloves, but I had a hand in it."
"How do you turn soup into gold? Add twenty-four carrots."
"I lost my mood ring. I'm not sure how I feel about it."

On its website, OneAmerica includes the signboards in the section on community service projects—and the categorization certainly seems appropriate.

46 AN EGG-CELLENT WAY TO TRAVEL

Which came first, the chicken or the limousine?

The most beloved vehicle in Indianapolis is not, surprisingly, a racecar. It's a limousine, painted bright yellow, with a giant chicken on top. When we spot it rolling down the street, we point and say, "Hey, look, it's the Chicken Limo!" Then we wave at whoever is lucky enough to be inside. A few years ago, an *Indianapolis Monthly* quiz about "how Indy you are" asked how you would respond if your significant other booked the Chicken Limo for a date. The correct answer: "Make sure it pulls up in front of your house so the neighbors can see." We just absolutely love this thing.

As often as I've spotted the Chicken Limo around town, I assumed there was a whole flock of kitschy yellow limos roaming the streets. But in fact there's only one Chicken Limo, and it's an Indy original. Owned by a local company called Specialty Limos, it is hugely popular for birthday parties (for both children and adults), prom nights, bachelor/bachelorette parties, weddings, pub crawls, or even just kooky joyrides. You don't *have* to show up in a chicken costume, but you wouldn't be the first.

Inside, the Chicken Limo seats eight and contains all the usual amenities: leather seating, a high-end sound system, coolers,

---

The Chicken Limo isn't just for humans: the vehicle once transported an entire flock of neglected chickens to a safe and comfortable foster home.

The Chicken Limo is an Indy original, and it's a popular choice for birthday parties, proms, weddings, and other special events. Photo courtesy John Barker.

and several TVs. But if that's not enough to entertain you, you can also ask the driver to make the chicken cluck or cock-a-doodle-do—which, as a bonus, is sure to get the attention of the neighbors.

THE CHICKEN LIMO

WHAT A yellow limousine with a giant chicken on top for no particular reason

WHERE Indy metro area

COST $75 to $100 per hour

NOTEWORTHY The Specialty Limos fleet also includes the purple Hippo Party Bus, which is almost—but not quite—as beloved as the Chicken Limo.

47 THE POWER OF LOVE

Why did Indy build a memorial to a five-minute speech?

When Martin Luther King Jr. was assassinated on April 4, 1968, riots erupted in more than one hundred cities across the nation. Indianapolis, however, remained relatively calm, and Robert F. Kennedy is given some of the credit. The Democratic senator was in Indianapolis that night, on the presidential campaign trail, and his speech encouraged a different kind of response.

Speaking in a local park, Kennedy began by telling the large crowd what had happened. "Martin Luther King dedicated his life to love and to justice for his fellow human beings, and he died because of that effort," Kennedy said. He told the crowd it was only natural to want to respond with violence—his own brother had been assassinated, and he too had struggled with bitterness, anger, and a desire for revenge. But, he said, "what we need in the United States is not division; what we need in the United States is not hatred; what we need in the United States is not violence or lawlessness; but love and wisdom, and compassion toward one another, and a feeling of justice toward those who still suffer within our country." Kennedy urged the crowd to go home and "say a prayer for our country and for our people." The next day, leaders in the African American community met with the mayor to discuss the racial inequality in the city (an issue that unfortunately persists today).

Robert F. Kennedy was assassinated in Los Angeles only two months after his memorable Indianapolis speech.

Located in Dr. Martin Luther King Jr. Park, the Landmark for Peace *sculpture depicts both King and Robert F. Kennedy. Then a Democratic presidential candidate, Kennedy gave a moving speech in the park on the day of King's assassination.*

LANDMARK FOR PEACE

WHAT A monument to compassion, love, and justice

WHERE Dr. Martin Luther King Jr. Park, 1702 N. Broadway St.

COST Free

NOTEWORTHY In 2018, on the fiftieth anniversary of Kennedy's speech, *Landmark for Peace* was designated as the Kennedy-King National Commemorative Site.

Located in the park where Kennedy spoke, the *Landmark for Peace* sculpture is a tribute to that moment. A groundbreaking ceremony for the memorial in 1994 was attended by President Bill Clinton, Senator Ted Kennedy, and two of King's sons. The steel sculpture depicts Kennedy and King reaching out to each other across a divide—a reminder for us to do the same.

48 A TUTU OR TWO

Why does Butler University own a famous collection of ballet costumes?

It would be hard to overstate the importance of the Ballet Russe de Monte Carlo. The classical dance company crisscrossed the United States on multiple tours in the 1940s and '50s, effectively introducing ballet to the masses, and it launched the careers of countless dancers. One of those dancers was George Verdak, who later served on the Butler University dance faculty. After the Ballet Russe folded in 1968, Verdak pulled some strings and arranged to have the troupe's legendary costumes donated to Butler.

Six of the Ballet Russe costumes—newly restored—are now on permanent display at the university's Schrott Center for the Arts. The exhibit includes tutus worn by two legendary prima

THE BALLET RUSSE DE MONTE CARLO COLLECTION OF THE BUTLER BALLET

WHAT A peek into the closet of a legendary ballet company

WHERE The Schrott Center for the Arts, Butler University, 4600 Sunset Ave.

COST Free

PRO TIP Butler Ballet's annual performance of Tchaikovsky's *The Nutcracker* is a holiday tradition for many Hoosier families.

Former Ballet Russe de Monte Carlo dancer George Verdak founded the Indianapolis Ballet Theatre, later called Ballet Internationale. It was the city's only professional ballet company at the time, but it folded in 2005 after thirty-two years.

These eye-catching costumes were created for the legendary Ballet Russe de Monte Carlo dance company, which folded in 1968. They are now on permanent display at Butler University's Schrott Center for the Arts. Photo courtesy Brent Smith/Butler University.

ballerinas, Maria Tallchief and Alexandra Danilova. Barbara Karinska, an Academy Award–winning costume designer, created several of the dresses on display. And the collection is beautiful even without the historical context.

Butler's collection also includes Ballet Russe scenery, such as backdrops from *Swan Lake*, *The Nutcracker*, *Scheherazade*, and the ballet version of *The Mikado*. The sets are too large for permanent display, but you might see one in use at a production by Butler Ballet. And your time will be well spent—Butler Ballet is consistently ranked as one of the top collegiate ballet programs in the nation.

49 THE GREAT SQUIRREL INVASION OF 1822

Why did a plague of rodents descend on Indianapolis?

If you've read Laura Ingalls Wilder's *On the Banks of Plum Creek* or perhaps the biblical book of Exodus, you know that a swarm of locusts can strip a field bare overnight. In 1822, farmers in Indianapolis had an equally devastating problem, except this time the culprit was squirrels.

Early settler Calvin Fletcher wrote, in a letter to his brother, that "the corn this year was literally destroyed . . . by gray and black squirrels." He reported that one man had killed nearly 250 squirrels in his cornfield without making a dent in their numbers. In *A Home in the Woods*, the memoirs of early settler Oliver Johnson as written down by his grandson, Johnson recalls that the squirrels came "by the thousands for several days." He and his family patrolled the fields with rifles by day and spent the nights molding fresh bullets.

To be fair, the squirrels invaded the cornfields that year because they were starving to death. The trees simply hadn't produced as many nuts as usual. Johnson recalled that "they was so starved and footsore from travelin that they wasn't fit to eat." As the squirrels migrated west, many farmers in the area lost their entire corn crop. It's a funny story in retrospect, but for a newborn Indianapolis the Great Squirrel Invasion of 1822 was a devastating blow.

Squirrels can't swim, but these invaders were undeterred by bodies of water. The squirrels at the front of the pack drowned, but the rest used their floating bodies as stepping stones.

During the Great Squirrel Invasion of 1822, thousands upon thousands of starving squirrels marched across the Midwest, searching for food. Unfortunately for local farmers, they found it in the cornfields of Indianapolis. Photo courtesy the Library of Congress.

THE GREAT SQUIRREL INVASION OF 1822

WHAT A plague of biblical proportions

WHERE A large swath of the Midwest

COST A fortune in corn (and the lives of many thousands of squirrels)

NOTEWORTHY Calvin Fletcher reported that a dozen squirrels could do as much damage as a single loose hog. We'll have to take his word for it.

50 A REAL HATCHET JOB

What activity has Indy borrowed from Canadian lumberjacks?

When you've had a bad day, there's nothing quite as satisfying as throwing sharp axes at giant wooden targets. And that's exactly what you can do at Bad Axe Throwing, which recently opened an Indianapolis venue. The company's mission is "to bring the thrill of a traditional Canadian backyard pastime to urban communities." The company operates thirty axe-throwing venues across the United States and Canada, and the new Indy venue has become a popular choice for adult birthday parties, team-building events, bachelor/bachelorette parties, and other get-togethers.

For your first visit, assemble a group of eight or more and book a private party. A coach will teach you basic throwing techniques and safety rules, and after some practice you'll split into two teams for some friendly competition. (My sisters and I still brag about beating the guys' team at my husband's birthday party.) For additional practice, you can take your chances with a walk-in session or book your own lane in advance—but slots fill up quickly, so chop chop.

Bad Axe Throwing also sponsors seasonal leagues, both recreational and competitive. The $15 weekly cost includes free walk-in practice sessions. Eventually, if you're sharp enough, you might even qualify for the World Axe Throwing League championship.

The Bad Axe Throwing website sells axes, target stencils, and shirts approved by the World Axe Throwing League.

Cinderblocks at Bad Axe Throwing hold axes of several different sizes and weights. If you book a private party, a coach will help you find the axe that's best for you—and teach you how to throw it properly.

BAD AXE THROWING

WHAT Cutting-edge entertainment

WHERE 235 S. Meridian St.

COST Cost: $24/hour for walk-in sessions; $39.25/person for private parties with a dedicated coach

PRO TIP Birthday parties booked at Bad Axe Throwing include free admission for the birthday person.

51 A PATHOLOGICAL HISTORY

Why does one Indy museum display dozens of human brains?

When Central State Hospital for the Insane was founded in 1848, the usual treatment for patients with mental illness was simply to lock them away. The new facility espoused a more compassionate view, believing that people with mental illness could be treated and even cured. To that end, the hospital established a pathology department in the 1890s, just as the medical profession was beginning to use the scientific method to pinpoint what caused disease. The hospital closed in 1994, but the Old Pathology Building lives on as the Indiana Medical History Museum, a fascinating relic of Victorian medicine.

The hospital's focus on mental illness is evident in the anatomical museum, where dozens of preserved brains are on display. Visitors generally wait in this room for tours to begin, but if you're particularly squeamish you can head straight through to the amphitheater. This is where doctors and medical students once observed autopsies and attended lectures. Next door is the formal autopsy room, where various medical gadgets are on display, such as antique wheelchairs and medical examining tables, a morgue refrigerator, and an iron lung designed for infants.

The tour also includes several laboratories—one for making slices of tissue and examining them under microscopes, for example, and another for examining blood with chemical tests. (The latter includes several antique centrifuges.) Other

---

Visits to the Indiana Medical History Museum are by guided tour only. They begin every hour, on the hour, and doors open ten minutes beforehand.

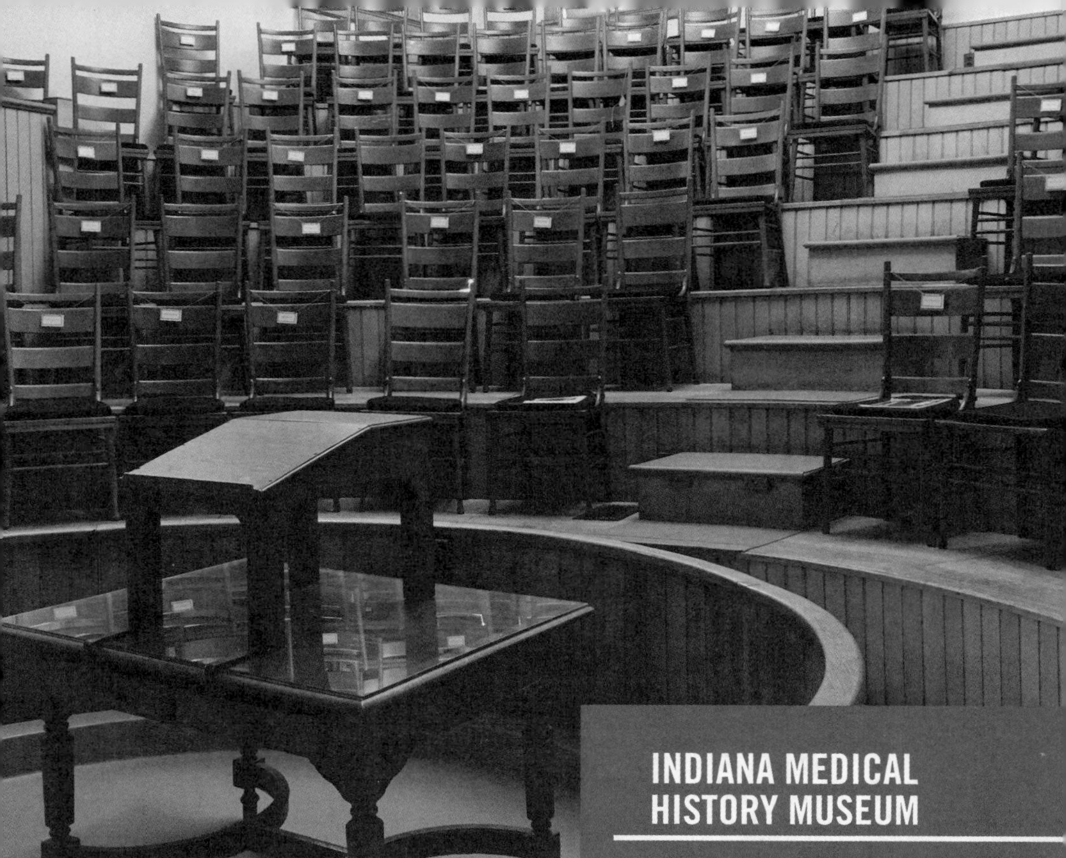

Tours of the Indiana Medical History Museum begin in the amphitheater, where medical students once gathered to hear lectures and observe autopsies. The room next door displays dozens of preserved human brains floating in jars.

INDIANA MEDICAL HISTORY MUSEUM

WHAT A pathology laboratory frozen in time

WHERE 3045 W. Vermont St.

COST $10

PRO TIP Leave younger children at home. The museum has a strict "do not touch" policy, and some of the subject matter might be disturbing for young visitors.

stops include a records room, a library, and an enormous camera for creating enlarged images of tissue samples.

By the 1960s, the Victorian pathology building was too outdated to meet the hospital's needs, and it was slated for closure. By then plans were already underway to turn the building into a museum, so the pathologists simply walked out and locked the doors behind them, preserving the facility exactly as it was.

52 THE BIG DIG

Why are Indy artists painting manhole covers?

All along the Indianapolis Cultural Trail, painted manhole covers celebrate an unusual goal: keeping raw sewage out of local waterways. Sponsored by Citizens Energy Group, the DigIndy Art Project is designed to beautify utilitarian manhole covers while also showcasing "what's going on below the surface."

Indianapolis built its sewers more than a century ago with a single goal in mind: to manage rainwater. As indoor plumbing became more common, however, sewage lines were simply hooked into the same pipes. And Indy's combined system still works just fine—except when it rains. Even a quarter-inch of rain can overwhelm the system, causing "combined sewer overflow" to spill into local waterways. Put another way, our rivers and creeks are sometimes full of raw sewage.

Understandably, the Environmental Protection Agency has asked cities with combined sewers to reduce overflow events. So, in 2012, Citizens Energy Group embarked on a massive project called the DigIndy Tunnel System. Located 250 feet below ground, the system will include twenty-eight miles of tunnels, all eighteen feet in diameter. By 2025, the tunnels will be able to store 250 million gallons of combined sewer overflow, thus keeping raw sewage contained until it can be treated.

In the 1950s, the Indianapolis Water Company (later sold to Citizens Energy Group) used the tagline "Everything that grows . . . *needs water!*" The slogan still appears on a vintage sign along Fall Creek Parkway.

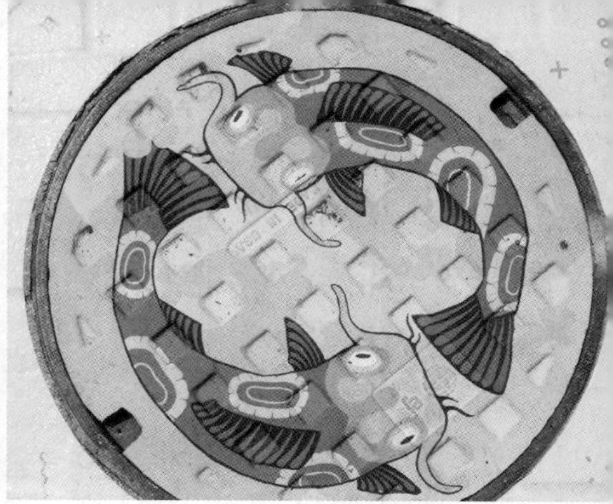

DigIndy MANHOLE COVERS

WHAT An unusual tribute to a modernized sewer system

WHERE Indianapolis Cultural Trail

COST Free

PRO TIP You'll find denser clusters of the painted manhole covers along Alabama and Washington streets.

Top left: *Artist, Merle Pace; location, Blackford Street at IUPUI.* Top right: *Artist, Mindy Whipple; location, Washington and Meridian streets.* Above left. *Artist, Christina Hollering; location: Alabama and New York streets. Photos courtesy Visit Indy.*

But how can you keep the public engaged in an infrastructure overhaul that will take more than a decade? The DigIndy Art Project is one attempt. Inspired by local waterways, the manhole covers depict fish, frogs, birds, turtles, local landscapes, and even a hybrid cat-mermaid.

53 THE DOWNFALL OF A BULLY

Who was James Overall, and why does his story matter?

The pariah of early Indianapolis was a man named David Burkhart, who called his followers the Chain Gang. He settled in the city around 1824 and soon "developed in depravity under the influence of whiskey," writes Jacob Piatt Dunn in his two-volume history of the city. When drunk, Burkhart went looking for a fight: he once got into a knife fight with a Methodist preacher and even a street brawl with the state treasurer. But his favorite victims were African Americans, whose homes he often vandalized.

One night in 1836, Burkhart and the Chain Gang attacked the home of James Overall, a prominent African American land speculator and church trustee. But Overall refused to stand aside as his home was ransacked. As they broke down the door, he fired his shotgun, wounding one man. The assailants fled, but Overall knew they would soon return for revenge. He sent word to attorney Calvin Fletcher, who later reported that he had assembled a constable and "a considerable number" of other prominent citizens to defend Overall against "the outrageous mob headed by Burkhart." They ordered Burkhart to leave town, immediately and permanently. And one Chain Gang member, David Leach, was arrested for breach of peace for shouting death threats during the incident.

James Overall's forgotten story of courage was rediscovered by historians studying the memoirs of travelers on the Underground Railroad, some of whom received help from Overall along the way.

This historical marker honors James Overall, one of the city's early African American settlers. It was erected in 2016 after researchers spent an entire decade arguing about whether to describe Overall's attackers as a "gang" or a "mob."

HISTORICAL MARKER FOR JAMES OVERALL

WHAT A reminder of one man's bravery

WHERE Near 524 N. West St.

COST Free

NOTEWORTHY A historical marker near the Indiana Landmarks Center honors a man named John Freeman, who fought successfully for his freedom in 1853 after being wrongly identified as a runaway slave.

Leach soon petitioned the court for release, claiming that his arrest was unlawful. According to Indiana law at the time, an African American could not testify against a white person in court. So, Leach asked, how could he be jailed based on Overall's testimony? The judge, however, ruled that Overall had a "natural" right to "avail himself of the remedies prescribed by law." It was a victory, but a fleeting one, and Overall's story was eventually forgotten. Nearly two centuries would pass before the Indiana Historical Bureau erected a marker in his honor.

54 THE OLD ORDER

Why does Holy Rosary still sometimes celebrate Mass in Latin?

The Catholic Church abandoned a centuries-old tradition in the 1960s, when the Second Vatican Council decreed that Mass should be celebrated in each church's local language rather than in Latin. Many Catholics welcomed the change, but some were nostalgic for the beauty and reverence of the traditional service. So, in the 1980s, Pope John Paul II gave permission for churches to celebrate the traditional Latin Mass, also called the Extraordinary Form and Tridentine Mass, in addition to the New Order of Mass. These days, however, only three churches in Indiana offer a Tridentine Mass, and the only local option is Our Lady of the Most Holy Rosary.

The early Catholic Church used Latin because it was the universal language at that time, but few people speak the "dead language" today. So why would anyone want to attend Mass in a language they don't understand? Proponents describe the service as reverential and beautiful—a vivid sensory experience enriched by Gregorian chants and the smell of incense.

Holy Rosary also celebrates the New Order of Mass, but the Extraordinary Form is offered at 11:30 a.m. on Sundays. It's a fascinating experience, even for non-Catholics, but it can also be somewhat confusing. The red missalettes in the pews contain

---

Holy Rosary Catholic Church was historically the parish of choice for Italian immigrants, and it is now best known for its annual Italian Street Festival.

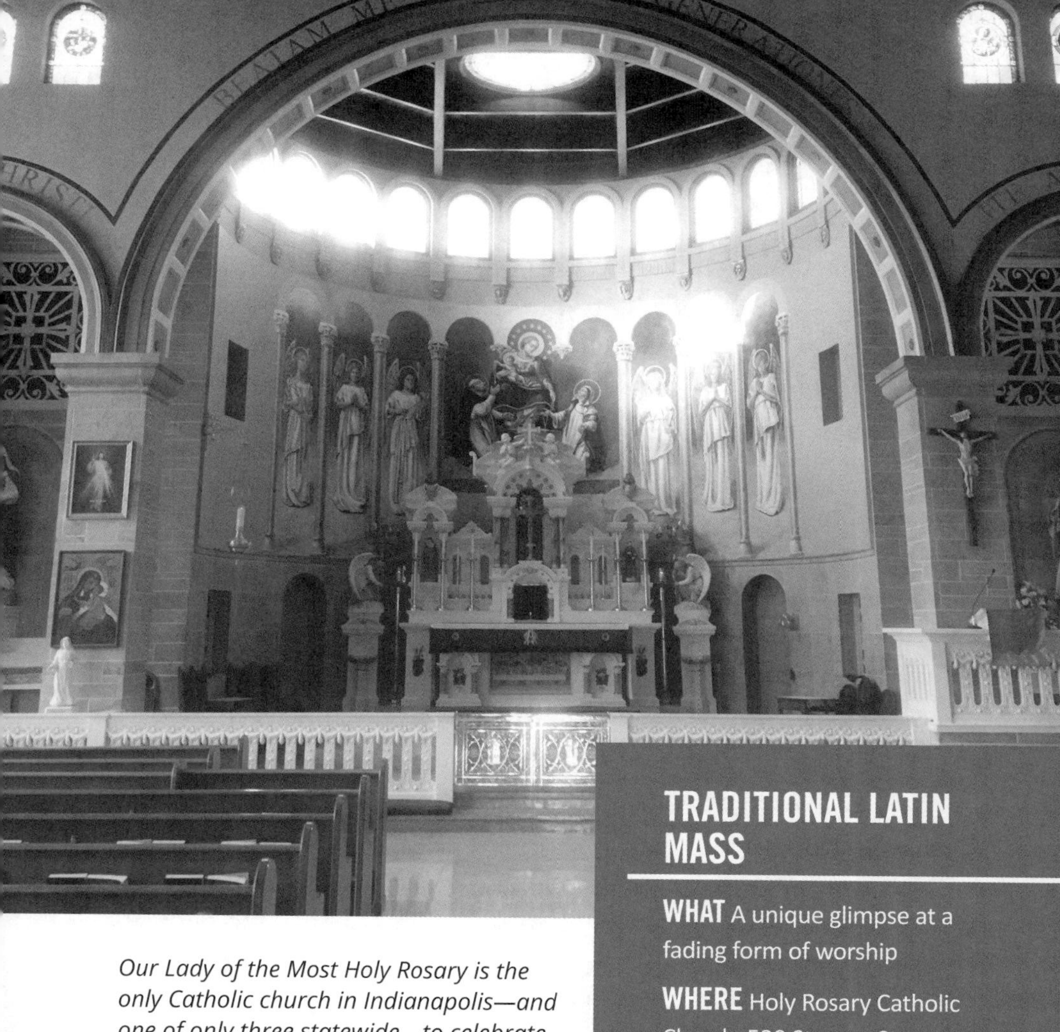

Our Lady of the Most Holy Rosary is the only Catholic church in Indianapolis—and one of only three statewide—to celebrate the traditional Latin Mass. Also called the Extraordinary Form and the Tridentine Mass, the service is offered at 11:30 a.m. each Sunday.

TRADITIONAL LATIN MASS

WHAT A unique glimpse at a fading form of worship

WHERE Holy Rosary Catholic Church, 520 Stevens St.

COST Free

PRO TIP Holy Rosary offers Latin courses for those who want to better understand the Tridentine Mass.

English translations, and handouts called Propers describe the prayers and readings for that particular day. Simply take your cues from the crowd about when to stand, sit, and kneel, and remember that communion is reserved for practicing Catholics.

55 A MAGNETIC MYSTERY

How can a car possibly roll up a hill?

Experiencing the eeriness of Mooresville's Gravity Hill requires just three simple steps: stop your car next to the culvert at the bottom of the big hill, put the car in neutral, and try to stay calm as the vehicle starts rolling *up* the smaller hill to the east. "Far as I know, it always worked," says Judith Walls in *More Amazing Tales from Indiana*. She once lived at the top of the hill, and she remembers nights when many cars would be lined up waiting their turn.

The story of Gravity Hill has been circulating for a century, practically since the first cars were on the road. One legend says cars are pushed uphill by a ghostly woman whose grandson was hit by a car, or perhaps by a ghostly group of children who died in a school-bus accident. Another story claims that a magical force field protects a hidden treasure buried nearby.

Alas, the truth is much less interesting. According to physics professors who have examined the site, it's just an ordinary optical illusion. But it's still fun to pour water on the road and watch it flow "uphill." Rolling a ball or soda can also works.

Kellar Hill is the spot's official name, and you'll find it southwest of Mooresville on Kellar Hill Road, about a mile west of State Highway 42. Note that the phenomenon only works if you're facing east. But it does work, and if you don't encounter traffic you can easily coast all the way back to 42.

GRAVITY HILL

On this stretch of Kellar Hill Road near Mooresville, cars defy the laws of physics by rolling uphill. Explanations for the Gravity Hill phenomenon range from an optical illusion to ghost stories and hidden treasures.

WHAT The perfect place to fight an uphill battle

WHERE Kellar Hill Road, Mooresville

COST Free

PRO TIP Roll at your own risk. This is a busy road, so it's essential to be cautious and alert.

Combine your Gravity Hill adventure with a meal at Gray Brothers Cafeteria. The Mooresville mainstay serves home-style favorites such as meatloaf and fried chicken.

56 A WHIRLWIND VISIT

Where can you view a huge collection of antique fans?

For more than a decade, the Antique Fan Collectors Association curated a museum of electric fans in Wichita, Kansas. But in 2008 the museum was forced to relocate, and the "only dedicated antique ceiling and desk fan museum in the world open to the public" soon whirred its way to Zionsville. It is now housed at Fanimation, a ceiling fan manufacturing company owned by AFCA member and avid collector Tom Frampton.

The fans here belong to AFCA members rather than the museum, and the members' pride is evident in the gleaming fan blades and careful restorations. More than two thousand fans are on display, including early fans powered by water, steam, alcohol, wind-up mechanisms, and belt-and-pulley systems. The collection represents more than 140 manufacturers, such as GE, Kenmore, and Westinghouse, and the oldest electric fans date to the 1890s. Some fans even come in unusual shapes, such as airplanes, windmills, chickens, and cats.

ANTIQUE FAN MUSEUM

WHAT The world's only museum of electric fans

WHERE 10983 Bennett Pkwy., Zionsville

COST Free

PRO TIP The museum has limited hours, weekdays only from 10 a.m. to 4 p.m.

The first floor focuses on antique tabletop fans; the second floor—which is easy to miss if you're not looking—has the ceiling fans and box fans. On both floors you'll find advertising memorabilia, including handheld fans promoting various businesses. You may even bump into AFCA members polishing up their collections. They'll be happy to tell you about their hobby, but be prepared for some fan-related puns.

More than two thousand antique fans are on display at the Antique Fan Museum in Zionsville. Curated by the American Fan Collectors Association, the museum bills itself as the only one of its kind in the world.

Here's a fun game to play at the Antique Fan Museum: Choose from dozens of identical remote controls and try to guess which ceiling fan you're about to turn on.

57 THE RIGHT KIND OF RAMEN

Which restaurant serves Indy's most authentic Japanese cuisine?

When you first spot Ichiban Noodles, you'll wonder how the family-owned restaurant stays in business. It's tucked away in a commercial area that gets zero pedestrian traffic and very little vehicle traffic. The sign is hand-painted. The building is sometimes described as a "shack." But the restaurant is often packed, and *Business Insider* recently named it the best ramen joint in the state. You'll understand why as soon as you taste the food.

Owners Louis and Nancy Hsu opened Ichiban Noodles in 2001. The restaurant specializes in Japanese cuisine, including sushi, bento boxes, tempura dishes, and noodle bowls—udon, ramen, and soba. If you're hoping for ramen just like the packaged stuff you ate in college, you'll be disappointed; the ramen here doesn't taste that way because it isn't supposed to. Loyal customers claim that it's the most authentic home-style Japanese cuisine in the city, and that there's even something special about the miso soup and green tea. The prices are low and the service is friendly, so dig in and try to overlook the perpetually half-finished renovation projects.

Note that the restaurant closes for a few hours between the lunch and dinner services (generally 2:30 p.m. to 4:30 p.m.).

The exterior of Ichiban Noodles may not look particularly inviting, but inside you'll find some of the best Japanese cuisine in the city. The menu offers dishes such as sushi, tempura, bento boxes, and noodle bowls.

ICHIBAN NOODLES

WHAT A home-style version of Japanese cuisine

WHERE 8355 Bash St.

COST Varies (budget friendly)

PRO TIP Check the address. This northside favorite is sometimes confused with Ichiban Sushi Bar, a similarly named restaurant (also with good sushi) on the opposite side of the city.

58 THE ART OF DECEPTION

How can a painting simply disappear before your eyes?

The Indianapolis Museum of Art is full of unexpected treasures. The gallery of contemporary design showcases bizarre furniture, vacuum cleaners, tea kettles, and even toilet-brush holders. The gallery of textile and fashion arts has glittering gowns by Halston, Bill Blass, Christian Dior, and Coco Chanel. And the gallery of contemporary art includes *Möbius Ship*, a large Möbius strip that is also—you guessed it—a model ship.

But the most startling piece in the museum's collection is *Acton*, by artist James Turrell. You'll find it in the gallery of contemporary art, set apart in a room of its own. Enter the dimly lit space and you'll see a large canvas painted a uniform dark gray. Not that interesting, right? But if you walk toward the painting, you'll soon experience a sudden shift in perception. *Acton* isn't a painting at all—it's a hole in the wall. Step backward, and it's a painting again. The optical illusion is so bewildering that viewers often reach through the hole, just to be sure.

The contemporary art gallery is also home to *Floor* by Korean artist Do-Ho Suh. As you walk across the glass surface, you'll see thousands of tiny spots of color below. But look more closely: those spots of color are the hands of thousands of tiny people, all working together to hold up the floor. Also look for the untitled sculpture by Tara Donovan that stands thirteen feet tall and resembles . . . a giant molecule, maybe?

According to the museum's catalog, artist James Turrell's goal with *Acton* was "to make the quality and sensation of light itself something really quite tactile."

ACTON BY JAMES TURRELL

The collection at the Indianapolis Museum of Art includes many unexpected treasures, such as vacuum cleaners, designer ballgowns, an army of tiny people, and a mind-boggling vanishing painting.

WHAT Artwork as optical illusion

WHERE Indianapolis Museum of Art, 4000 Michigan Rd.

COST $18 for adults, $10 for kids

PRO TIP Don't miss Winterlights, a popular holiday event where the museum grounds are decorated with millions of beautiful outdoor lights.

59 A ROOM WITH A VIEW

What secret awaits you in the City-County Building?

The City-County Building isn't exactly a tourist destination. In 1974, a *New York Times* article called the building "faceless and anonymous," declaring that "its consummate dullness [was] almost a negative achievement." But there's a secret hiding on the twenty-eighth floor: an observation deck that offers one of the best views in the city.

The observation deck is open to the public, but it's a bit tricky to find. After you get through security, look for the service elevator with the red doors. Inside you'll find an honest-to-goodness elevator operator, who has been running this elevator since 1981 (she took over when the building's first elevator operator retired). She will deliver you to the twenty-sixth floor, where you'll wait for yet another elevator—this one much smaller—to take you up the final two floors.

Here is the withering critique in its entirety: ". . . a new City–County headquarters that looks as if someone had pushed a computer button marked 'Standard Speculative Office Building.' Faceless and anonymous, its consummate dullness is almost a negative achievement. It successfully suggests that beyond the reality of business as usual, there are no longer any large dreams or aspirations, or even any authority in the government process to be respected or expressed through design."

—Ada Louise Huxtable, *New York Times*

The observation deck on the twenty-eighth floor of the City-County Building offers a 360-degree view of the Circle City.

CITY-COUNTY BUILDING OBSERVATION DECK

WHAT A bird's-eye view of the city

WHERE 200 E. Washington St.

COST Free

PRO TIP The observation deck has limited hours: 10 a.m. to 3 p.m., weekdays only.

The city could do a lot more with this space. The exhibits at the center of the room are neglected, and clearly afterthoughts. But you're not here for the exhibits; you're here for the views. Check out Monument Circle and the Statehouse, and remind yourself how enormous Lucas Oil Stadium actually is.

The City-County Building isn't the tallest in the city, but it's not far behind. For people who are new to the city, this is the perfect way to get oriented. And even for lifelong Indy residents, it's fun to see a familiar city from a new perspective.

60 THE URBAN BUZZ

Where in Indy can you get an education in beekeeping?

To qualify as an entry-level urban homesteader, all you need is a vegetable garden, a compost pile, and a backyard full of chickens. The intermediate level involves adopting a couple of goats and a llama, with bonus points if you make your own pickles. But to reach the elite level of urban homesteading, what you really need is your very own backyard beehive.

The recent resurgence of beekeeping is good news for the Beekeepers of Indiana, which runs the annual Indiana Bee School. The course for beginning beekeepers is capped at two hundred people, and it reliably sells out every year. Beginners learn about topics such as bee biology and nutrition, hive inspection, and bee-friendly landscaping. Experienced beekeepers, meanwhile, can expand their skillset with topics such as selling honey; making creamed honey; and brewing mead, a honey-based wine. Vendors at the Indiana Bee School sell all kinds of bees, naturally, as well as basic equipment and supplies. Also on offer are honeybee insurance, insemination devices, hive-monitoring equipment, and nutritional supplements—yes, actual vitamins designed just for bees.

Bee populations are declining nationwide, but urban beekeeping could be part of the solution. Surprisingly, city bees tend to be healthier than country bees, probably because they are exposed to fewer pesticides.

At the annual Indiana Bee School, novice beekeepers learn about topics such as bee biology and nutrition, hive inspection, and bee-friendly landscaping. Photo courtesy the Beekeepers of Indiana.

INDIANA BEE SCHOOL

WHAT Everything you need to know about urban beekeeping

WHERE Various locations

COST $50

PRO TIP The Beekeepers of Indiana also runs a Young Beekeeper Program, which is open to children twelve and older.

If you're not quite ready to commit to Bee School, try visiting the large Beekeepers of Indiana booth at the Indiana State Fair instead. There you can chat with experienced beekeepers, sample and buy honey from across the state, attend beekeeping presentations, and observe a beehive in action. But be careful: you may find yourself signing up for Bee School the moment you taste the honey ice cream.

61 AN OFFICER AND A GENTLEMAN

Why did Confederate soldiers erect a monument to a Union officer?

Two years before the Civil War, Indiana purchased a beautiful new site in the countryside for the State Fairgrounds. Part of the present-day Herron-Morton Place neighborhood, it was bordered by Nineteenth and Twenty-Second streets and Central and Talbott avenues. But when the war began in 1861, Governor Oliver Morton designated the fairgrounds as a military training camp for thousands of Hoosier volunteers, and it later became a prison camp for Confederate soldiers.

The first camp commandant was Colonel Richard Owen, a man who balanced strong discipline with kindness and compassion. At first the camp was chaotic—it needed, for example, a hospital and a kitchen capable of feeding thousands of men. But Owen made sure the prisoners had good food, warm clothes and blankets, and medical attention, and he instituted a system of self-government among the prisoners that became a model for other camps. He also allowed them to form glee clubs, dramatic societies, and sports leagues. Prisoners praised Owen in their letters home, and word of his kindness spread throughout the South.

Owen was deployed later that year, and afterward camp conditions declined dramatically. Smaller rations, dreadful medical care, and overcrowding escalated the number of deaths and escape attempts. Owen, however, was repaid for his

---

The bust of Col. Richard Owen was created by sculptor Belle Kinney, a Tennessee native whose father had been a Confederate soldier.

Col. Richard Owen served as the first commandant of Camp Morton, a prison camp for Confederate soldiers during the Civil War. Half a century later, Confederate veterans honored his kindness with this bust in the Indiana Statehouse. Photo courtesy Bass Photo Co. Collection, Indiana Historical Society.

MEMORIAL TO COLONEL RICHARD OWEN

WHAT A touching tribute to wartime kindness

WHERE Indiana Statehouse, 200 W. Washington St.

COST Free

PRO TIP Don't miss the beautiful stained-glass ceiling in the statehouse rotunda. It is made from German glass and is original to the 1888 building.

efforts. When he was captured in Kentucky a few months later, the Confederate general thanked him for his kindness to the prisoners and set him free.

In 1911, a group of Confederate veterans collected donations to memorialize Owen with a small bronze plaque. But so much money poured in that they were able to upgrade their plans. They instead commissioned a large bronze bust of Owen, which now sits in the Indiana Statehouse. The inscription reads, in part, "Tribute by Confederate prisoners of war and their friends for his courtesy and kindness."

62 THE ODDNESS OF OTTERNESS

How did Indy acquire its cutest grouping of public art?

Just outside the Indiana Convention Center, two teensy tourists gawk at an enormous couple dancing on a giant bag of money. The three bronze sculptures are called *Male Tourist, Female Tourist*, and *Free Money*, and the roly-poly grouping manages to be both deftly satirical and completely adorable.

The sculptures are a legacy from *Tom Otterness in Indianapolis*, a citywide exhibition in 2005 that featured twenty-five sculptures by the world-renowned artist. Curated by the Arts Council of Indianapolis, it was the largest public art exhibition in city history. And the whimsical figures—such as a fish wearing a tiny hat and a beaver using his cellphone—were an instant hit. After the exhibition closed, a group of private donors contributed more than $550,000 to bring the trio back to Indy for good.

Like *Free Money*, many of the sculptures in the 2005 exhibition commented on social inequality. A giant penny crushed tiny people as it rolled along, while other tiny people danced precariously on top. A piece called *Miser* depicted a large man standing astride a globe, handing out mere pennies to the little people below. But a companion piece nearby, called

FREE MONEY, MALE TOURIST, AND *FEMALE TOURIST*

WHAT Three whimsical reminders of a beloved exhibition

WHERE 499 W. Maryland St.

COST Free

PRO TIP Another sculpture by Tom Otterness, called *Boy and Dog*, lives on the southeast corner of St. Clair and East streets. Although this is private property, it's okay to take a closer look; Otterness stipulated in the purchase agreement that the sculpture remain accessible to the public.

The trio of Tom Otterness sculptures near the Indiana Convention Center weighs a combined 4,200 pounds.

These bronze sculptures at the Indiana Convention Center were created by world-renowned artist Tom Otterness. They first came to Indy in 2005 as part of the citywide Tom Otterness in Indianapolis *exhibition, the largest of its kind in city history.*

Educating the Rich on Globe, showed the miser smooshed flat by a woman reading a book.

Locations for the 2005 exhibition were carefully chosen—a large bear at the Indianapolis Zoo, for example, and a covered wagon at the Eiteljorg Museum of American Indians and Western Art. A sculpture called *Mad Mom* was placed in front of the statehouse, much to everyone's delight. The current location of Indy's sculptures follows that tongue-in-cheek pattern, placing *Male Tourist* and *Female Tourist* next to a convention center that is generally full of tourists.

63 THE HERALD OF SPRING

Where in the city can you picnic with Persephone?

Butler University has a closely guarded secret. Holcomb Gardens, the campus greenspace, is a favorite retreat for students, faculty, and staff, but the university doesn't publicize its hidden gem. It mentions the gardens on the website only to suggest them as a potential wedding venue. But don't let that stop you from exploring.

The twenty-acre park is heavily wooded, and it has walking trails, a small pond, and waterfalls. It is also home to a garden house, a gazebo, and the Holcomb Memorial Carillon Tower. Quotes from great thinkers, such as Socrates and Gandhi, are inscribed on the philosopher's bench, and the poet's corner features quotes from Shakespeare, Wordsworth, Tennyson, and others. But the highlight of Holcomb Gardens is the grass mall, which stretches five hundred feet along the Indianapolis Greenway Canal. The lawn is flanked by hedges and trees, and its dominant feature is an 1840 statue of Persephone by French sculptor Armand Toussaint.

According to the Cultural Landscape Foundation, Holcomb Gardens was designed in 1949 by James Holcomb, then a university trustee, and Arthur Lindberg, the superintendent of buildings and grounds. Construction was completed a year later. The carillon tower was added in 1959 as a memorial to Holcomb's wife, Musetta.

Butler University's Holcomb Observatory and Planetarium is one of the largest public observatories in the world. Planetarium shows and public tours are available most weekends when classes are in session.

HOLCOMB GARDENS

WHAT A calming campus retreat

WHERE Butler University, 4600 Sunset Ave.

COST Free

NOTEWORTHY The newest addition to Holcomb Gardens is the Thomas E. Willey Memorial Rock Garden, which honors a former history professor.

This 1840 statue of Persephone lives in Holcomb Gardens, a hidden gem at Butler University. The plinth reads, in part, "In ancient Greek mythology, she, as the daughter of Zeus and Demeter, was worshipped as the goddess of vegetation, returning each spring from the realm of Hades to herald the season of growth, and in winter disappearing to pass her time, like the seed, under the earth." Photo courtesy Brent Smith/ Butler University.

Holcomb Gardens is on the north side of campus, stretching up to Fifty-Second Street. It is bounded by the canal to the west and a cluster of athletic facilities to the east, and it can be accessed from either campus or the Canal Towpath. If you go during spring break or other school vacations, you just might have the beautiful gardens to yourself.

64 THE INDUSTRIAL ARTS

How are artists reusing the city's abandoned factories?

Between the trendy restaurants and the shiny new apartments, it's getting harder and harder to find art galleries and studios in traditional enclaves such as Mass Ave and Fountain Square. So where have all the artists gone? One answer is the city's former factories.

Take, for example, the Circle City Industrial Complex. Built in the 1920s, the building was originally a manufacturing facility for the Schwitzer Corporation, which made auto parts such as cooling fans and water pumps. Now the 500,000-square-foot facility houses more than fifty artist studios and galleries, as well as a brewery and a seasonal farmers' market.

The Stutz Business and Arts Center has a similar story. Built between 1912 and 1919, it was once the primary manufacturing facility for the Stutz Motorcar Company. The complex has 400,000 square feet and takes up an entire city block. The forbidding exterior hasn't changed much over the years, but the complex now has studios for more than eighty artists, designers, architects, and other creative professionals. It bills itself as the "largest group of artists under one roof in the Midwest."

In contrast, the Tube Factory Artspace was never used for auto manufacturing. But the Garfield Park building, now an art gallery and community center, previously served as a dairy bottling

---

Indy's arts scene is buzzing about Art Dish, a new monthly dinner series at the Harrison Center for the Arts. The event combines talks by the gallery's exhibiting artists with themed dining experiences prepared by the city's best chefs.

This playful mural at the Tube Factory Artspace depicts the building's former industrial uses as a dairy bottling facility, peanut roaster, and manufacturer of metal tubes. Many of Indy's abandoned factories are finding new life as arts venues.

facility, a peanut roaster, and of course a tube factory.

Other industrial facilities have found new life as event spaces. A former factory for windows and doors is now the Biltwell Event Center, and Crane Bay once produced potbelly stoves and train engine components. But some, like the former Ford assembly plant on Washington Street, will simply be reborn as more apartments.

FACTORIES TURNED ARTS ENCLAVES

WHAT A creative re-use of Indy's abandoned industrial spaces

WHERE Circle City Industrial Complex: 1125 Brookside Ave.; the Stutz: 212 W. Tenth St.; Tube Factory Artspace: 1125 Cruft St.

COST Varies, but usually free

PRO TIP More than sixty studios are open to the public during the Stutz Artists Open House each April.

65 A TOUR WITH A TWIST(ER)

What happens behind the scenes at the National Weather Service?

Where does thunder come from? How do tornadoes form? Why is rain made of water instead of meatballs? If your kiddos have been asking these questions—or if you've always wondered about them yourself—it may be time for a tour of the local National Weather Service Forecast Office.

The NWS, then known as the US Weather Bureau, established its first Indianapolis office in 1871, on the southeast corner of Washington and Meridian streets. The office was relocated many times over the years; the current office on Hanna Avenue opened in 1993. Every day meteorologists there collect vital readings such as temperature, humidity, precipitation, atmospheric pressure, and wind speed.

Tours begin in the operations area, where visitors see the tools NWS forecasters use to predict the weather, including satellite and radar imagery and computer modeling. Tour guides discuss NOAA Weather Radio, which airs local weather information around the clock. They also explain the NWS system for issuing severe weather warnings. The tour may also include a visit to the WSR-88D—a fancy name for the Doppler radar—and a discussion of basic weather observation skills. Visitors might even

---

One of Indy's worst weather-related disasters was the Great Flood of 1913, when some neighborhoods were submerged under thirty feet of water. But the exact height of the flood crest is unknown—the gauge was swept away.

NATIONAL WEATHER SERVICE FORECAST OFFICE

WHAT A rare peek into the wonders of weather

WHERE 6900 W. Hanna Ave.

COST Free

PRO TIP Tours must be scheduled in advance; contact the office at (317) 856-0360 or w-ind.webmaster@noaa.gov.

On a private tour of the National Weather Service Forecast Office, you'll learn about the tools and technologies that meteorologists use to predict the weather and to monitor potentially dangerous weather events.

meet staff members with unusual titles such as "service hydrologist" and "hydro-meteorological technician."

Tours typically last about an hour, and the maximum group size is twenty. Many visitors come on school field trips, but families and other small groups are also welcome.

66 ANOTHER BOATLOAD OF KNOWLEDGE

Where in landlocked Indy can you earn a sailing certification?

There are no ropes on a sailboat. There are lines, stays, shrouds, sheets, halyards, and topping lifts, but nothing that's just called a rope. This is one of the first lessons you'll learn at Dauntless Sailing School, which runs classes on Geist Reservoir from spring to fall.

The school's six-week beginner course covers fundamentals such as terminology, safety procedures, sail trim, anchoring, docking, and basic navigation. Experiential learning is key, so all classes take place aboard the twenty-eight-foot *Dauntless*. By the end of the course, you and the rest of the crew will be setting sail with minimal guidance. The good news: It's nearly impossible to capsize a boat like the *Dauntless*, and so far no student has gone overboard. The bad news: Geist Reservoir is actually quite shallow, so if you stray too far off course you might run the boat aground. Or you might, as I once did, nearly crash the boat into a dock. It's all just part of the learning process.

Captain Todd Bracken launched the school in 2009, and the adult beginner sailing course is the most popular offering. But more advanced students can earn a skipper certification or take courses in coastal navigation, and supplementary online

---

To sail Geist Reservoir without committing to a semester of classes, book a spot on a sunset sailing cruise. Dauntless Sailing School offers 2.5-hour tours on Friday evenings in summer, at a cost of $49 per person.

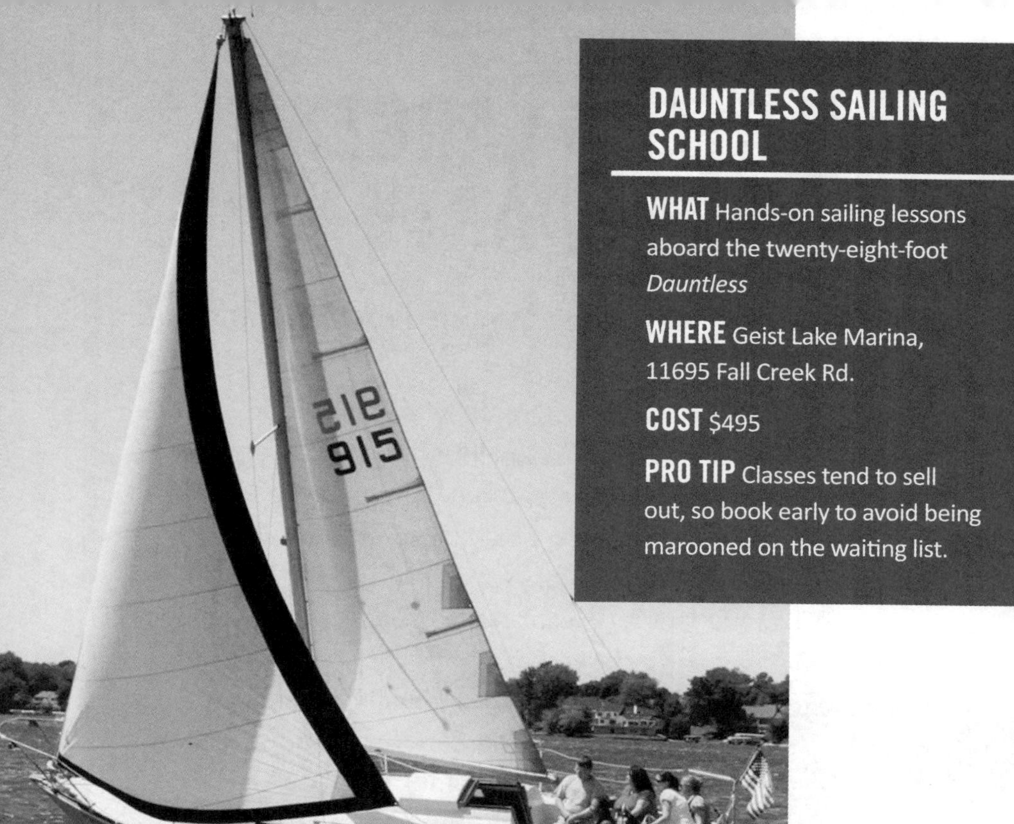

DAUNTLESS SAILING SCHOOL

WHAT Hands-on sailing lessons aboard the twenty-eight-foot *Dauntless*

WHERE Geist Lake Marina, 11695 Fall Creek Rd.

COST $495

PRO TIP Classes tend to sell out, so book early to avoid being marooned on the waiting list.

Dauntless Sailing School emphasizes hands-on learning, even for absolute beginners, so all classes are taught aboard the Dauntless *on Geist Reservoir. Photo courtesy Dauntless Sailing School.*

coursework is available through NauticEd. Students can also create an online logbook to track their sailing hours and build a resume—an important document for those who want to eventually charter a boat.

Bracken also organizes regatta participation and group excursions for students and alumni who want additional practice. Excursions include everything from overnight trips on Lake Michigan to week-long coastal cruising expeditions all over the world.

67 THE CITY'S LARGEST COSTUME PARTY

Where can you wear your Dumbledore outfit and still fit right in?

Each year in early August, the streets of downtown Indy get decidedly weird, crawling with superheroes, Star Trek aliens, Jedi knights, Pokémon characters, and uniformed students from Hogwarts. But locals don't bat an eye—it's just the sixty thousand attendees at Gen Con, which bills itself as "the largest annual consumer fantasy, electronic, sci-fi, adventure, and hobby game convention in North America."

Founded fifty years ago in Lake Geneva, Wisconsin (thus the name), Gen Con has called Indy home since 2003. The heart of the event is the vendor hall, where attendees can try out the year's most anticipated new tabletop games. But that's just the beginning. A recent convention schedule included nearly 18,000 gaming events, including 6,500 related to board games; 4,400 related to

GEN CON

WHAT The epicenter of cosplay and tabletop gaming

WHERE Indiana Convention Center, 100 S. Capitol Ave.

COST $110 for a four-day badge, plus optional extras

PRO TIP Cosplay opportunities also abound at Indiana Comic Con, an annual gathering focused on comic books.

I once attended a Shakespeare performance at White River State Park that was interrupted by a giant Pikachu wandering through the audience. That's just life in Indy during Gen Con.

You don't have to wear a costume to the annual Gen Con gaming convention, but how else will you win the costume contest? Photos courtesy Gen Con, LLC.

role-playing games; and more than a thousand related to card games. There's also a live-action dungeon experience, fierce robot battles, film screenings, art exhibits, crafting sessions, celebrity meet-and-greets, playtests of prototype games, and (of course) a costume parade.

But the breadth of Gen Con's offerings is perhaps best displayed by its educational seminars. Topics that same year included Norse mythology, leatherwork, cosplay photography, ballroom dance, global pandemics, interstellar travel, the publishing process, negotiation strategies, steampunk, and 3D printing techniques. Attendees could even learn how to wear a kimono or build eye mechanisms for a puppet. In other words, it's impossible to do everything at Gen Con—so no wonder gaming fans keep coming back.

68 THE SPEEDWAY'S SECRET LEGACY

How did a former "Millionaires Row" become a Catholic university?

It seems sacrilegious to write a book about Indianapolis without mentioning the Indy 500. Yet the world's largest single-day sporting event hardly qualifies as a secret. Neither do related destinations, such as the Indianapolis Motor Speedway Museum and the Dallara IndyCar Factory. Fortunately, an Indy 500 secret is hiding in plain sight at Marian University, where two historic mansions have little-known ties to the "greatest spectacle in racing."

The Indianapolis Motor Speedway was founded in 1909, and the inaugural Indy 500 came two years later. Three of its founders were Carl Fisher, James Allison, and Frank Wheeler. Soon after, the three men also became neighbors.

Allison, with Fisher as his partner, had made his fortune with the Prest-O-Lite Company, and he later founded what became the Allison Division of General Motors. Construction on the Allison Mansion began in 1911 and cost about $2 million, with a Gothic library, a Louis XVI reception room, Tiffany stained-glass ceilings, and Italian marble floors. Fisher, meanwhile, purchased the existing house next door. Wheeler started construction on his own mansion in 1912. It wasn't quite as glitzy, but it did have a seven-car garage. The home was later owned by G. Monty

---

After co-founding the Indianapolis Motor Speedway, Carl Fisher went on to establish a new Florida resort community. You know it as Miami Beach.

Indianapolis millionaire James Allison built this mansion—now on the campus of Marian University—soon after co-founding the Indianapolis Motor Speedway. Completed in 1914, the $2 million home was known for a time as "the House of Wonders." Photo courtesy the Library of Congress.

THE MARIAN MANSIONS

WHAT Home sweet home for the founders of the speedway

WHERE Marian University, 3200 Cold Spring Rd.

COST Not open to the public

NOTEWORTHY The Stokely-Wheeler Mansion has a covered walkway the length of a football field. It was designed for walking the family dogs in inclement weather.

Williams, CEO of the Marmon Motor Company—another speedway connection, as Ray Harroun won the first Indy 500 driving a Marmon Wasp.

All three estates were eventually subsumed by Marian University. Fisher's home was gutted by fire, but the Allison Mansion lives on as an event venue and the office of the university president, and the Wheeler home houses the admissions department. Although the buildings aren't open to the public, you're free to wander the campus of the former Millionaires Row.

69 A SHORT TRIP AROUND THE WORLD

Where in Carmel can you travel from the Seine to the Southwest?

If you expect the Museum of Miniature Houses to be full of dollhouses, you're right . . . sort of. These exhibits are definitely not playthings for children—rather, they are true works of art, many by Indiana artists, with intricate details you could examine for hours. In addition to complete dollhouses and diorama-like "room boxes," the museum also displays collections of tiny furniture, dolls, and housewares.

THE MUSEUM OF MINIATURE HOUSES AND OTHER COLLECTIONS

WHAT A museum of fine art in miniature

WHERE 111 E. Main St., Carmel

COST $10

PRO TIP The museum is located in the Carmel Arts and Design District, which has a wealth of options for shopping and dining.

Peek into a tiny art studio along the Seine, explore the rich details in Sherlock Holmes's apartment, browse a frontier trading post, or spin the 360-degree display of a contemporary California mansion. You'll even find a few LEGO figurines, along with room boxes depicting a greenhouse, a roadside souvenir shop in Arizona, a toy shop, a general store, a carpenter shop, and a museum. And don't miss the miniature French chateau, which is decorated

---

Most of the displays at the Museum of Miniature Houses are created on a 1:12 scale—one inch of dollhouse for every twelve inches in real life.

This may look like a cozy Nantucket cottage, but it's actually a dollhouse with historically accurate furnishings and decor. Created by artist Pam Throop, it's on display at Carmel's Museum of Miniature Houses and Other Collections.

with crystal chandeliers, fine paintings, and richly upholstered furniture. The museum has more miniatures than it can display at one time, so exhibits are rotated frequently—meaning there's something new to see every time you visit.

70 A PLACE TO STEW

How can an under-the-radar restaurant also be "famous"?

Only a tiny handful of Indianapolis restaurants have survived for a century or more, and many residents can rattle off the list: the Slippery Noodle (1850), the Rathskeller (1894), St. Elmo Steak House (1902), Shapiro's Delicatessen (1905), and Workingman's Friend (1918). But even locals tend to forget John's Famous Stew, which traces its history back to 1911.

The restaurant was founded by two brothers, Steve and Mike Strangeff, Macedonian immigrants who gambled everything on their mother's beloved recipe for stew. For Dapa Strangeff, who used giant iron kettles and wood-burning stoves, the stew had simply been a practical way to feed nine children and the farm's many field hands. The restaurant has moved several times over the years, from Washington Street to South Street to Kentucky Avenue, but Mother Strangeff's stew is still the highlight of the menu.

JOHN'S FAMOUS STEW

WHAT An often-overlooked centenarian

WHERE 1146 Kentucky Ave.

COST Varies

PRO TIP The daily specials are comfort food at its finest: chicken and noodles, country-fried steak, meatloaf, pork chops, and more, usually served with a side of mashed potatoes and gravy.

Not in the mood for stew? John's Famous Stew also serves burgers, steaks, sandwiches, salads, and beef or turkey manhattans drowning in gravy.

Since its founding in 1911, John's Famous Stew has showcased a traditional stew recipe from Macedonia. The hearty stew takes three hours to cook and is still made from scratch every day. Stew photo courtesy John's Famous Stew.

The stew is made from scratch every day, in five-gallon batches, and cooks for about three hours. The giant stirring paddle would also be very handy in a canoe. The stew comes in mild, medium, and spicy varieties, and it's packed with beef, potatoes, and veggies such as carrots and celery. Each order comes with bread to sop up the leftover gravy. If that doesn't sound like enough food, you can instead order the "supreme" version, which is served atop a breaded pork tenderloin. But don't forget to leave room for an order of house-made cobbler.

71 AN ENGINE FOR CHANGE

How is a local arts collaborative transforming a south-side community?

The Big Car Collaborative can be hard to explain. Essentially, the nonprofit organization uses the arts as a tool to build communities. And, since Big Car's founding in 2003, that mission has fueled an enormous variety of projects. The list includes pop-up art galleries, offbeat performances, neighborhood markets, community gardens, mural projects, film screenings, and "placemaking activations" in historic downtown spaces. The organization has created bus stop shelters, mobile libraries, neighborhood signage, and a mobile park on wheels. It runs an affordable housing program for local artists, and its Listen Hear project champions sound as an artistic medium. Big Car has transformed a restroom into an art gallery and curated exhibitions of ping-pong tables, Bigfoot evidence, and art inspired by kitchen appliances. It is also the local coordinator for the 48 Hour Film Project. And that's not even the whole list.

Big Car was based for many years in Fountain Square, and its presence was transformative for that neighborhood. Now the collaborative is bringing that same energy to Garfield Park, where it recently invested $1.5 million to transform a vacant

---

The unusual putt-putt hole at the Tube Factory Artspace honors Dick the Bruiser, a professional wrestler from Indiana. It was originally part of an interactive exhibit at the Indianapolis Museum of Art, in which artists designed eighteen holes for a putt-putt course celebrating Indiana history.

Located in Garfield Park, the Tube Factory Artspace uses inviting outdoor spaces to engage with the community. The former factory now houses workshops, a community art center, and a decidedly quirky art gallery.

TUBE FACTORY ARTSPACE

WHAT A new life for a forgotten industrial building

WHERE 1125 Cruft St.

COST Free

NOTEWORTHY The Tube Factory Artspace property is also home to a bee sanctuary and a fair number of chickens.

industrial building into the Tube Factory Artspace. Inside are workshops, event spaces, a reference library, a community art center, and an art gallery with ever-changing exhibitions. The space has limited hours on evenings and weekends, but it's open until 10 p.m. on First Fridays. Stop by to see . . . I mean, who knows? With Big Car, anything is possible.

72 QUACK IN THE PULPIT

How was Indy once connected with a cult in Guyana?

Indianapolis has many dark secrets, but one of the darkest is its connection to a notorious cult leader. Jim Jones, who was born near Richmond, moved here to begin his ministry in 1951. He soon began offering bogus faith healings that captivated crowds. And in 1954 the charismatic leader founded his own church, Community Unity, later known as the Peoples Temple Full Gospel Church.

Jones left a mixed legacy in Indianapolis. He was an early champion for racial integration, even serving as chair of the Indianapolis Human Rights Commission. His church operated a soup kitchen that served three thousand meals every month. But he was also running a tax-evasion scheme to funnel money to the church. He claimed to have powers of psychic discernment and prophecy, and he systematically isolated church members from their families.

In 1965, Jones prophesied a nuclear war that would destroy both Chicago and Indianapolis, and he led his congregation to a new home in California. But he couldn't stay ahead of the bad press and legal investigations forever, and in 1977 Jones and his followers fled to Guyana. When US Representative Leo J. Ryan of California visited the Jonestown compound the following year, attempting to escort home some would-be defectors, he and several reporters were gunned down by Jones's guards. Jones

---

Jim Jones raised money for his first church by importing monkeys from South America and selling them door to door for $29 apiece. He ultimately sold about 1,700 monkeys to Indy residents.

Jim Jones poses for a photo in 1956, two years after founding his Indianapolis church. The dapper reverend in the bowtie would eventually become one of history's most notorious cult leaders. Photo courtesy the Indianapolis Recorder Collection, Indiana Historical Society.

RESTORATION BAPTIST CHURCH

WHAT The former home of the notorious Peoples Temple

WHERE 1502 N. New Jersey St.

COST Free

NOTEWORTHY Charles Manson, another charismatic but dangerous man, is also from Indiana.

knew it was the end. On his orders, the entire congregation—more than nine hundred people—committed a mass murder-suicide by drinking Kool-Aid laced with cyanide. Many of the victims were children.

One of the former Peoples Temple church buildings still stands in Indianapolis, offering a glimpse into a haunting history. It now houses Restoration Baptist Church, which has no affiliation with Jones's ministry.

73 A BRUTAL ARCHITECTURAL LEGACY

Who designed the city's ugliest building?

The two federal buildings in downtown Indianapolis couldn't be more different. The Birch Bayh Federal Building on Ohio Street is a classical Beaux Arts beauty, but nobody would use the word *beautiful* in reference to the Minton-Capehart Federal Building. It may actually be the most reviled building in the city.

Built in 1975, the Minton-Capehart building houses the local offices of the IRS, the Veterans Administration, and the Social Security Administration, among others. The "inverted ziggurat" structure was built in the Brutalist style and looks something like a stack of automobile air filters. A vibrant mural by Milton Glaser, called *Color Fuses*, wraps around the base of the building, but it is overshadowed—literally—by the hulking slabs of concrete above it. For this monstrosity we can thank a local architectural firm, Woollen Associates (later Woollen, Molzan & Partners, and now defunct). To be fair, the building does have its defenders. Jordan Ryan, an architectural archivist with the Indiana Historical Society, notes the intentional contrasts between the building and its surroundings. The architect "noticed all of the vertically emphasized structures around the plaza—the World War Memorial just to the south, the obelisk across the street, even the Scottish Rite beyond the plaza," she said. As a contrast,

---

Woollen Associates, the architectural firm that designed the Minton-Capehart Federal Building, was also responsible for Barton Tower—another Brutalist construction that Hoosiers love to hate.

The Minton-Capehart Federal Building, pictured here in 1976, is the city's most controversial example of Brutalist architecture. Photo courtesy the Indiana Historical Society, M1221.

MINTON-CAPEHART FEDERAL BUILDING

WHAT An eyesore of Brutalist architecture

WHERE 575 N. Pennsylvania St.

COST Free

NOTEWORTHY Milton Glaser, the graphic designer who created the building's mural, is best known for designing the iconic "I♥NY" logo.

"he made a conscious effort to emphasize the horizontality of the Minton-Capehart structure." Likewise, the "inverted ziggurat" structure is an upside-down echo of the ziggurat atop the war memorial.

The firm's Brutalist ethos in the 1960s and '70s wasn't all bad: it also gave us Clowes Memorial Hall. In later years, the Woollen firm built a reputation for historic preservation, restoring Union Station, the Indiana Repertory Theatre, City Market, the Majestic Building, and Christ Church Cathedral. By the time it folded in 2011, it had—perhaps—repaid its debt to society.

74 THE HOOSIER POET

Where in Indy did James Whitcomb Riley live?

At the peak of his popularity in the early 1900s, James Whitcomb Riley was known as both "the Hoosier poet" and "the children's poet." His folksy rhymes written in a backwoods dialect were beloved throughout the nation, and it was Riley, along with contemporaries such as Booth Tarkington and Gene Stratton-Porter, who first put Indiana literature on the map. Unfortunately, Riley's poetry hasn't aged particularly well. Modern readers may struggle to appreciate a poem such as "Granny," which begins thus:

> Granny's come to our house,
> And ho! My lawzy-daisy!
> All the childern round the place
> Is ist a-runnin' crazy!

But Riley's legacy lives on in the nationally ranked Riley Hospital for Children and the Riley Children's Foundation. Without him, Indianapolis would be a very different place.

The James Whitcomb Riley Museum Home—one of the best-preserved late-Victorian homes in the nation—gives fans a glimpse into the poet's daily life. Born in nearby Greenfield, Riley moved here in 1893 as a paying boarder. The luxurious Italianate mansion was among the first in the city to have indoor plumbing, and Riley spent his years here in comfort. Soon after his death in 1916, the home was purchased and preserved by his friends

---

The Raggedy Ann doll was invented in Indianapolis, and her name was inspired by two of James Whitcomb Riley's poems: "The Raggedy Man" and "Little Orphant Annie."

At the James Whitcomb Riley Museum Home, fans of the Hoosier Poet's folksy rhymes can see many of his possessions, including his signature pince-nez glasses. This bust in the side yard was designed to stand at Riley's exact height.

JAMES WHITCOMB RILEY MUSEUM HOME

WHAT A peek into the life of a Hoosier poet

WHERE 528 Lockerbie St.

COST $4

PRO TIP Serious Riley fans should also visit his grave in Crown Hill Cemetery and the James Whitcomb Riley Boyhood Home and Museum in Greenfield.

and fans, so all the objects on display actually belonged to Riley and the family who owned the home. These include Riley's book collection; his pince-nez glasses, top hat, and cane; a portrait of his dog, Lockerbie; and even his shaving razors. His writing desk is scarred with burn marks from his cigars. It seems as if Riley might come strolling through the door at any minute, with Lockerbie at his heels, and pick up where he left off.

75 ODDBALL ATHLETICS

Why does Indy have so many unusual sports leagues?

Back when Indy was known as Naptown, city leaders staked the community's future on amateur sports. And it worked. Now the "amateur sports capital of the world" is home to a variety of athletic organizations. And the emphasis on amateur sports has trickled down to local recreational leagues, which offer a surprising array of offbeat fitness opportunities.

Circle City Athletics, which coordinates leagues for "social sports," offers such options as pickleball, dodgeball, and bocce ball. Indy is also the birthplace of linear bocce, which is played in back alleys with plenty of booze—mostly by current and former staffers of *The Indianapolis Star*, although the public is welcome too. The Indianapolis World Sports Park has facilities for cricket, which is odd because nobody here plays cricket. The axe-throwing leagues at Bad Axe Throwing are covered elsewhere in this book. And other recreational options include the Indianapolis Fencing Club; the Table Tennis Club of Indianapolis; and Indy Synchro, a synchronized swimming team. Meanwhile, the Indy Cycloplex has facilities for BMX and cyclocross events, as well as one of the only operating velodromes in the nation.

Each year the city hosts the linear bocce world championships—a slight overstatement given that linear bocce

---

Athletes at the Indianapolis Scottish Highland Games are required to wear kilts whenever they are on the field.

Practice makes perfect for Indy Synchro, a local synchronized swimming team. Other unusual recreational leagues across the city focus on axe throwing, pickleball, fencing, and linear bocce. Photo courtesy Kristen Wells.

is a decidedly local phenomenon. IUPUI holds an annual canoe race along the canal downtown. And athletes at the annual Indianapolis Scottish Highland Games toss around stones, giant poles, metal balls, and burlap bags stuffed with straw. So Indiana may be basketball territory, but here in Indy you have plenty of other options.

UNUSUAL SPORTS LEAGUES

WHAT Quirky alternatives to the office softball league

WHERE Various locations

COST Varies

NOTEWORTHY The velodrome at the Indy Cycloplex is named for Indy native and legendary cyclist Marshall "Major" Taylor. Born in 1878, he faced overwhelming prejudice as an African American athlete. But he set numerous world records, won dozens of major races, and eventually claimed a world championship.

76 HISTORY, REPEATING ITSELF

Which museum lets you step right into historical photographs?

The Indiana Historical Society was founded in 1830, only fourteen years after Indiana achieved statehood. So you might assume that its beautiful building on Ohio Street is a dusty repository for faded photographs, yellowing newspapers, genealogical records, and antique books. The Indiana History Center does have all those things, but more importantly it's a museum of state history, and the exhibits are surprisingly immersive and engaging.

The award-winning "You Are There" exhibit series, for example, brings historic photographs to life with costumed actors and hands-on activities. One exhibit re-creates a 1939 archeological dig at Angel Mounds, highlighting topics such as the Great Depression, archeological tools and techniques, and the prehistoric Mississippian culture that once thrived in the area. Another exhibit, set in 1839, introduces you to the denizens of a frontier inn during a time of religious upheaval. The Destination Indiana gallery puts you at the helm of a time machine, where you can explore more than three hundred stories from Indiana history. The Cole Porter Room re-creates a 1940s cabaret, and the interactive History Lab focuses on conservation techniques. Special events include Oregon Trail simulations, a circus festival, musical performances, scavenger hunts, storytelling events, and evening tours paired with themed cocktails. So go learn to juggle, and try not to die of dysentery.

The History Lab is one of many interactive experiences at the Indiana History Center. Visitors can also step into 3D re-creations of old photos, travel across the state in a "time machine," and catch live performances in the Cole Porter Room. Photo courtesy the Indiana Historical Society.

INDIANA HISTORY CENTER

WHAT An immersive journey through Indiana's past

WHERE 450 W. Ohio St.

COST $9 for adults, $5 for kids

PRO TIP For more immersive Indiana history, spend a day at Conner Prairie. The interactive history park in Fishers was the first Smithsonian affiliate in the state.

The Indiana History Center has one of the city's best gift shops, the Basile History Market. On the lower level, the Stardust Terrace Café is a convenient lunch option, with plenty of seating along the scenic Central Canal.

77 A ROMAN HOLLIDAY

Why does an Indy park have fake "ancient" ruins?

In the eighteenth century, English landscape gardens often had at least one folly—a beautiful and expensive building that served no practical purpose. And, in a way, Holliday Park has a folly of its own: a unique sculptural installation called the Ruins that mimics the crumbling ruins of Italy and Greece.

The strange story of the Ruins begins in New York City. On the façade of the St. Paul Building—one of the city's first skyscrapers—were three large sculptures collectively known as *The Races of Man*. Sculptor Karl Bitter had drawn inspiration from the mythological Atlas, and the three stooped figures appeared to be working together to hold up the building. But their labors came to an end in 1958, when the Western Electric Company slated the building for demolition.

The company wanted to find a good home for the sculptures, which were then valued at $150,000. So it launched a design competition, asking cities to submit proposals for putting the statues on permanent display. Indy's winning plan mimicked the façade of the St. Paul Building,

THE RUINS AT HOLLIDAY PARK

WHAT A clever and quirky rehoming

WHERE 6363 Spring Mill Rd.

COST Free

PRO TIP Holliday Park also has a network of walking trails and one of the best playgrounds in the city.

Carmel's Flowing Well Park has an unusual feature of its own: a natural underground reservoir that spouts fifteen gallons of water every minute. The water is safe to drink, so fill up a few containers to take home.

The Ruins at Holliday Park were designed to showcase three large sculptures, called The Races of Man, *that had previously graced the façade of a New York skyscraper. After years of neglect, the Ruins were finally refurbished in 2016.*

thus placing the statues in their original context. And perhaps Indy got some extra credit because the statues were carved from Indiana limestone.

The true folly of this story is that Indy hasn't always given the Ruins the love they deserve. Design disputes and construction snags delayed the dedication for years, and the park once considered dismantling the Ruins to make way for a nature center. Eventually years of neglect transformed the fake Ruins into actual ruins. Thankfully, the site finally got a makeover in 2016, complete with new water features, a tree-lined promenade, lots of seating, and exquisite landscaping. So pack a picnic basket and go see Indy's folly as it was always meant to be.

78

AN OCEAN OF INFORMATION

Which local library has a portal to the South Seas?

In 1924, an Indianapolis accountant read a book that changed his life. The accountant was William F. Charters, who made his living investigating unreported assets for tax purposes. The book was *White Shadows in the South Seas*, a memoir by Frederick O'Brien about his travel experiences in French Polynesia. O'Brien described a rich culture that he felt was critically endangered by Western contact, and which would eventually leave behind "no written record save the feeble and misunderstanding observations of a few alien observers" (presumably excepting himself).

Charters was deeply moved by what O'Brien had written. He began collecting books that documented the cultures of the South Seas, focusing on primary accounts written by early explorers, missionaries, and travelers. When he donated the collection to Butler University six years later, it included more than two thousand volumes—meaning Charters had collected at the rate of nearly one book every day. It remains the largest collection of its type in the continental United States. It includes a rare 1622 book by Sir John Hawkins about his 1593 privateering venture in the South Seas, but generally Charters didn't waste money on fancy first editions—unlike other book collectors, what he cared about was content. The collection includes some highly questionable titles, such as *Life and Laughter Midst the*

The first special collection donated to Butler University was from natural history professor David Starr Jordan in April 1877. It was his collection of preserved fish.

This engraving of a Hawaiian dancer was printed in A Voyage to the Pacific, *a 1784 book by John Webber about British explorer James Cook. The book is one of thousands in the William F. Charters South Seas Collection at Butler University. Image courtesy Butler University.*

WILLIAM F. CHARTERS SOUTH SEAS COLLECTION

WHAT One man's feverish project of cultural preservation

WHERE Irwin Library, Butler University, 4600 Sunset Ave.

COST Free

NOTEWORTHY William F. Charters limited his collection to books written in English, presumably because he wanted to actually read them. But he did make exceptions for dictionaries written in the area's indigenous languages.

Cannibals, but Charters ultimately succeeded in his mission. His books document many aspects of South Seas culture, such as songs, oral traditions, religious ceremonies, and arts and crafts, that otherwise would have been lost. Your South Pacific adventure awaits in the Special Collections and Rare Books Room at Butler's Irwin Library.

79 A HOME FOR GNOMES

How does a bizarre collection honor a baker's homeland?

When Juergen Jungbauer opened the Heidelberg Haus in 1968, he decorated the German bakery and café with familiar items from his homeland. Garden gnomes were an obvious choice, given their reputation in Germany for bringing good luck and warding off evil. Five decades later, more than five hundred gnomes have taken up residence at the Heidelberg Haus. And, on the annual Sunshine and Fresh Air Day, every single gnome is taken outside to the parking lot for a tally.

Yet somehow the kitsch never overshadows the kitchen at this unique eatery. Display cases in the bakery section are stocked with Black Forest cake, German chocolate cake, soft pretzels, fruit strudels, seasonal springerle cookies, and other tempting treats. The small café offers the same sixteen-item menu it served on opening day, primarily sausage dishes such as bratwurst, knockwurst, and kielbasa. The potato salad—made with bacon, onions, and vinegar, but no mayo—is a local favorite.

The bakery selection reflects Jungbauer's extensive training as a pastry chef, starting with an apprenticeship at age fourteen. He built his resume at the upscale hotels of Europe and then immigrated to the United States in 1963. His plans went temporarily awry when he was drafted into the Army, but soon his superiors discovered his talents. They were eager to generate some good publicity for the military,

HEIDELBERG HAUS

WHAT A unique German café, bakery, and gift shop

WHERE 7625 Pendleton Pike

COST Varies (budget friendly)

PRO TIP If you're known for gnomes, don't miss the gnome festival held each spring at Garfield Park Conservatory. You can even lend your own gnomes for the display.

The Heidelberg Haus, a German café, bakery, and gift shop on the east side, is decorated with hundreds of whimsical garden gnomes. Owner Juergen Jungbauer is originally from Germany, where gnomes are said to bring good luck.

so they entered Jungbauer in cooking competitions across the country; his winning streak made him a local celebrity.

There isn't much seating at the Heidelberg Haus, so you may have to wait for a table. In the meantime, take some fun photos with the exterior murals, which depict an idyllic German countryside. And there's plenty to see in the gift shop: beer steins, springerle molds, imported foods, vintage VHS tapes, toys, candy, and every imaginable kind of German knickknack. And, of course, gnomes.

When a car crashed into the Heidelberg Haus in June 2016, the Jungbauer family set up "gnome triage" and costumed the gnomes with eye patches and bandages.

80 A BITTER THEATRICAL RIVALRY

What's the story behind the anchor of Fountain Square?

For an inspiring story of survival, look no further than the Fountain Square Theatre. The theater opened in 1928, toward the end of the city's theatrical building boom, and from day one it had a fierce rival. The Granada Theatre had opened across the street only a month earlier.

Coincidence? Not at all. As Howard Caldwell relates in *The Golden Age of Indianapolis Theaters*, an anonymous theater chain had attempted to purchase the Fountain Square Theatre during its construction. The offer was refused, and "within weeks someone started building what supposedly was to be an apartment on the opposite corner," Caldwell writes. In reality it was the Granada, built by the Universal theater chain—perhaps out of pure spite. The Granada had a Spanish theme, and the Fountain Square Theatre had an Italian theme, but otherwise they were virtually identical. But the Fountain Square Theatre eventually emerged victorious, and the Grenada closed in 1951.

The victory was short-lived, however. Doomed by its declining neighborhood, the Fountain Square Theatre closed in 1960. The building housed a Woolworth's store and lunch counter for part of the 1960s, and later a used furniture store and thrift shop.

Friday night swing dances at the Fountain Square Theatre kick off at 8:30 p.m. with a live jazz orchestra. But beginners should arrive an hour earlier for the dance lesson, a bargain at just $2 extra.

When the Fountain Square Theatre opened in 1928, it immediately had to contend with a rival theater that had recently opened nearby. But the Fountain Square Theatre outlived its competitor; that building is now the Murphy Arts Center. Photo courtesy the Bass Photo Co. Collection, Indiana Historical Society.

FOUNTAIN SQUARE THEATRE

WHAT A true survivor

WHERE 1105 Prospect St.

COST Varies

PRO TIP For duckpin bowling, reservations are essential.

Eventually, though, the neighborhood's fortunes were revived by an influx of artists and entrepreneurs, and restoration work on the building began in 1993.

Today the Fountain Square Theatre is once again a thriving cultural center. It is one of the few venues in the Midwest for duckpin bowling, a vintage version of the game with smaller balls and pins. The theater also hosts weekly swing dances, and the building houses a small inn, several restaurants, and a rooftop cocktail bar. So, essentially, it's a perfect weekend getaway. You'd never even need to leave the building.

81 A TRULY MONSTROUS MANSION

What's the story behind the wacky house on Kessler Boulevard?

Growing up, my friends and I called it "the Mafia house." The bizarre home on Kessler Boulevard is a sprawling 29,500 square feet, with oddly shaped windows, elaborate lighting, a quarter mile of curving balconies, and a huge dolphin fountain in the front yard. In retrospect, members of the Mafia probably wouldn't want such a showy house. But who would build such a thing?

The answer is Jerry Alan Hostetler, a former pimp known to police as Mr. Big. In the 1960s he started a construction business and purchased a small ranch house on Kessler. But it didn't stay small for long. He added new wings and outbuildings, connecting them to the main house with glass walkways. When the lot was full, he built new stories onto the existing buildings. Then he began to buy neighboring houses, which he connected to the main house. At its largest, the house had roughly fifty rooms (even Hostetler wasn't quite sure). Inside were a stone grotto, a ballroom, dozens of chandeliers, and a huge collection of art—all in questionable taste.

But Hostetler couldn't afford to maintain the house, and the foreclosures began—foreclosures, plural, because every

---

When the Hostetler house first hit the market, the property listing went viral. The *New York Post* called it "the ugliest house in America," and Curbed declared that "absolutely everything is wrong with this Indiana house."

This bizarre mansion was once a modest ranch house. Jerry Alan Hostetler, who was known to the police as Mr. Big, spent decades enlarging the house and buying up surrounding homes to connect to the main building. At press time it was once again for sale.

THE HOSTETLER HOUSE

WHAT A bizarre architectural landmark

WHERE 4923 Kessler Blvd. E. Dr.

COST Not open to the public

NOTEWORTHY At press time the house was listed for $998,000, with seven bedrooms, seven full baths, and 29,500 square feet.

neighboring lot had been purchased with a separate mortgage, and Hostetler had defaulted on only some of them. He eventually moved out, and he died in 2006.

Since then, owners have struggled to find a purpose for the house. The Baha Men, of "Who Let the Dogs Out" fame, once stayed at the house for several weeks, and it briefly served as the setting for an entrepreneurial boot camp. One family tried actually living there but found it impractical. So, for now, Hostetler's boondoggle sits in limbo.

82 THE BEST IN CLASS

What's the history of the city's public high schools?

In the midst of debates about school funding and standardized testing, we often forget that the city's public high schools have a rich and fascinating history. The story starts in 1864 with the founding of Indianapolis High School, the first free public high school in the state. Later renamed Shortridge High School, the school has a long list of notable alumni, including writers Booth Tarkington, Kurt Vonnegut, and Dan Wakefield. And no wonder, given that the *Shortridge Daily Echo* was the first daily student newspaper in the nation.

Shortridge was the only public high school in the city until Emmerich Manual High School opened in 1895. According to the *Encyclopedia of Indianapolis*, it was one of the first high schools in the nation to embrace the concept of manual training. That philosophy soon spread to Arsenal Technical High School, which opened in 1912 on the seventy-six-acre campus of a former Civil War arsenal.

At first the city's high schools served students of all races. But in the 1920s the Ku Klux Klan wielded enormous political power in Indianapolis, and the school board was pressured to create a segregated high school for African American students. Crispus Attucks High School opened in 1927. It was always overcrowded and underfunded, and until the 1940s it was barred from membership in the Indiana High School Athletic Association. When the school won its first state basketball championship in

---

For a closer look at the historic Arsenal Tech campus, head to the Colonel's Cupboard. The restaurant is operated by students in the Culinary Arts Program and is housed in a historic 1870 residence on the property.

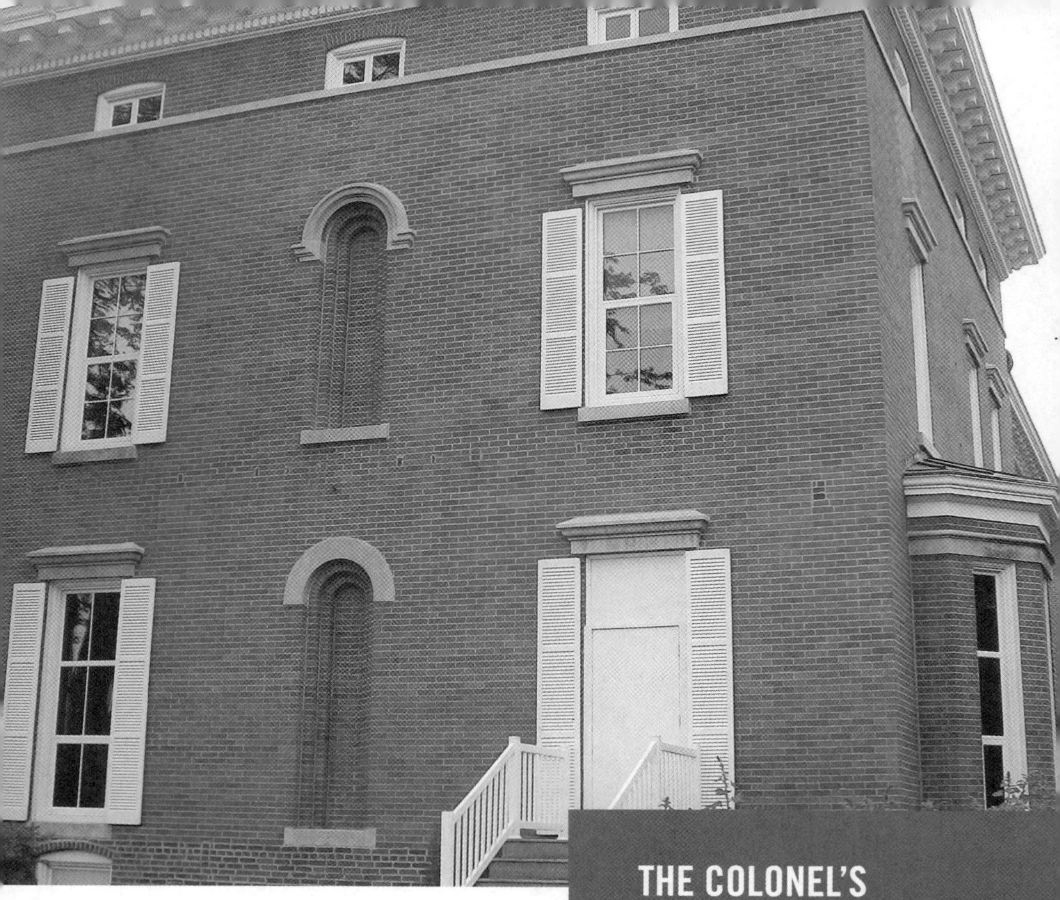

A student-run restaurant called the Colonel's Cupboard now occupies the historic West Residence at Arsenal Technical High School. The school opened in 1912 on the grounds of a former Civil War armory. Photo courtesy Wikimedia Commons.

THE COLONEL'S CUPBOARD

WHAT A student-run restaurant on a historic high school campus

WHERE Arsenal Tech, 1500 E. Michigan St.

COST Varies (budget friendly)

PRO TIP The media center houses a small museum assembled for the school's recent centennial.

1955, it was the first all-black high school in the nation to win a state title in any sport. It was also the first state basketball championship for a team from Indianapolis, which must (I hope) have greatly vexed the city's segregationists.

Access to public schools is limited these days, but check the Indianapolis Public Schools calendar for open houses and other community events.

83 A SHOT AT VICTORY

Which NCAA athletes literally aim for greatness?

The National Collegiate Athletic Association, which is headquartered in Indianapolis, sanctions twenty-four collegiate sports. You definitely know about crowd favorites such as football and basketball. You may even know about lower-profile sports such as bowling and water polo. But you probably don't know about rifle, which has the lowest profile of any NCAA sport. It's also one of only three NCAA co-ed sports (the other two are fencing and skiing).

During an NCAA rifle match, five team members each get 120 shots—sixty with a smallbore rifle (from fifty feet away) and sixty with an air rifle (from thirty-three feet away). The challenge demands mental focus, careful breath control, and a practiced trigger squeeze. The best of the best hit the bullseye 98.5 percent of the time in smallbore and 99.8 percent of the time in air rifle—pretty impressive considering that the bullseye is the size of the period at the end of this sentence. The four highest individual scores in each round count toward the team's aggregate score.

You can learn more about the NCAA's most obscure sport by visiting the rifle exhibit at the NCAA Hall of Champions. One of the items on display is a rifle team uniform from Texas Christian University, which made history in 2010 when it became the

---

The Children's Museum of Indianapolis offers another option for sports-related fun. Its indoor/outdoor Sports Legends Experience, which opened in 2018, lets kids climb trees, meet legendary athletes, and try out a dozen different sports.

This exhibit at the NCAA Hall of Champions highlights the organization's most obscure sport—and one of only three co-ed NCAA sports. On display is a uniform from the first all-female rifle team to win the national championship. Photo courtesy NCAA Hall of Champions.

first all-female squad to win the national championship.

The Hall of Champions also has exhibits for the other twenty-three sanctioned NCAA sports, with plenty of games, sports simulators, and video highlights to keep the kiddos entertained.

RIFLE EXHIBIT AT THE NCAA HALL OF CHAMPIONS

WHAT A tribute to a lesser-known collegiate sport

WHERE 700 W. Washington St.

COST $5 for adults, $3 for kids

PRO TIP Combine a visit to the NCAA Hall of Champions with stops at other cultural attractions in White River State Park, such as the Indiana State Museum, the Eiteljorg Museum of American Indians and Western Art, the Indianapolis Zoo, and Victory Field.

84 THE BEAT OF A DIFFERENT DRUMMER

What exactly is a museum of percussive arts?

You can make a tremendous amount of noise at the Rhythm! Discovery Center, banging on gongs, cymbals, marimbas, and every imaginable kind of drum. Yet somehow the museum of percussive arts leads a quiet existence, and even many locals don't know it exists. If you haven't yet explored this noteworthy museum, it's time to get your groove on.

The Rhythm! Discovery Center is a project of the Percussive Arts Society, which is headquartered here in Indy, and it opened its doors in 2009. Start your visit by banging the eight-foot gong near the entrance, and then explore interactive exhibits dedicated to the science of sound, basic drumming techniques, and percussion instruments from many different cultures and time periods. You'll see drum sets once played by famous musicians, as well as novelty instruments that would be right at home in a Dr. Seuss story—think boobams, Buzz-a-Phones, Timbracks, and Waterphones.

Your visit concludes in the interactive Groove Space, where you could spend hours trying out the hundreds of different percussion instruments. Join a drum circle, rattle a tambourine, or claim a soundproof practice room and make as much noise as you please (or just hide from your kids for a couple of minutes).

RHYTHM! DISCOVERY CENTER

WHAT An interactive museum of percussion

WHERE 110 W. Washington St.

COST $12 for adults, $6 for kids

PRO TIP Special events include group music lessons, community drum circles, and live performances by local musicians.

The Rhythm! Discovery Center uses hands-on activities, such as drum circles, to teach visitors of all ages about the art and science of percussion. Photo courtesy Rhythm! Discovery Center/Amanda Reynolds Photography.

Go behind the scenes at the Rhythm! Discovery Center with a private tour of the collection storage space. The "Behind the Glass" tours highlight many rare and unique musical artifacts that aren't on public display.

85 THE KING OF INDY BREWS

What secret experience awaits at the Sun King tasting room?

Sun King Brewery is hardly a secret. Its beers, such as the Sunlight Cream Ale and Pachanga Mexican-Style Ale, are available across the state and beyond. And twice Sun King has persuaded the state legislature to increase the annual volume cap for breweries, simply so it wouldn't have to halt production mid-year.

The company's main brewing facility is a popular downtown hangout, and many beer enthusiasts have taken the guided behind-the-scenes tour of the brewing and canning process. The tour costs $10 and includes samples of all five core Sun King beers. But the secret here is the reserve tour. It costs twice as much, but it includes parts of the facility that most visitors never get to see. The itinerary includes the full regular tour, plus a visit to the barrel-aging facility and rare samples of King's Reserve barrel-aged and sour beers. You might get to try Diddy Muckle, a Scottish-style ale aged in a bourbon barrel; the Velour Soccer Mom, a sour ale aged on raspberries and hibiscus; or any other brew on Sun King's long list of seasonal and limited-edition beers. A souvenir tasting glass is included in the price, and other Sun King merchandise is available in the gift shop. If you've

---

In addition to its main brewing facility downtown, Sun King operates a taproom and small-batch brewery in Fishers and a distillery in Carmel.

Sun King Brewery's downtown tasting room offers two behind-the-scenes experiences. One is a basic tour of the brewing and canning facilities. The other is the reserve tour, which offers exclusive access to the barrel-aging facility and rare samples of limited-edition barrel-aged and sour beers.

planned ahead for a designated driver, stick around after the tour for the sample flights: $8 will get you six samples of anything on tap in the tasting room.

RESERVE TOUR AT SUN KING BREWERY

WHAT A rare look at Sun King's limited-edition brews

WHERE 135 N. College Ave.

COST $20

PRO TIP Sun King offers discounted growler refills on Fridays, dropping the price for a half-gallon growler from $8 to $6.

86 THE LITERARY ARTS

Which miniature Indy library is located inside a refrigerator?

Libraries often contain works of art, but the mission of the Public Collection is to transform works of art into libraries. Since 2015, the project has installed a dozen "book share stations" across the city, all designed by Indiana artists. The Indianapolis Public Library keeps the stations supplied with books—eighty thousand of them and counting. And the stations aren't monitored, so readers are free to borrow, return, trade, and donate books at their own pace.

Monument Circle is home to the most visible Public Collection miniature library. The eighty-foot span of steel columns, painted a vivid green, was designed by Brian McCutcheon. A beam across the top, connecting the columns, bears a quote from Mark Twain: "A public library is the most enduring of memorials, the trustiest monument for the preservation of an event or a name or an affection; for it, and it only, is respected by wars and revolutions, and survives them."

Brose Partington designed the motorized library at City Market, which references the industrialization of agriculture. And Tom Torluemke created a bookshelf disguised as a refrigerator for the Hawthorne Community Center; the piece is called *Cool Books, Food for Thought*. Other book share stations include an

---

The mission of the Public Collection project is threefold: to improve literacy, to foster a deeper appreciation for the arts, and to promote social and educational justice.

PUBLIC COLLECTION MINIATURE LIBRARIES

WHAT A growing series of artist-designed "book share stations"

WHERE Throughout the city

COST Free

NOTEWORTHY The Public Collection initiative was developed by local philanthropist Rachel M. Simon, a graduate of the Herron School of Art and Design.

Designed by Katie Hudnall, this miniature library was installed at Eskenazi Health in 2015 as part of the Public Collection initiative. The piece, called Nautilus, *is a loose interpretation of a boat. Hudnall says it is "designed to remind the viewer that books (and education in general) can be a form of transportation."*

abstract topiary, a curvy cedar house, a LEGO sculpture, and two giant question marks. Several other miniature libraries are currently in the planning stages, so visit the Public Collection website, www.thepubliccollection.org, for project updates and a handy map.

87 A QUICK JAUNT TO JAMAICA

Where in Indy can you find Jamaica's version of fast food?

The loyal customers at Patties of Jamaica are in on one of the city's best-kept secrets. The Caribbean restaurant is off the beaten track, tucked away in a strip mall at the corner of Fifty-Second Street and Allisonville Road. It is closed on weekends, and the tiny dining area has only two tables. But the restaurant has survived since the early '80s on the brisk carryout business for its specialty, Jamaican patties.

The restaurant was founded by Henry and Theresa Seung, both born and raised in Jamaica, and the menu was built around the foods they missed most after moving to the United States. It is now run by their son, Stefan, and his wife, Jerusha, who churn out hundreds of patties by hand every day.

A Jamaican patty is essentially a hand pie; it may be a colonial descendant of a British pasty. The flaky pastries are stuffed with seasoned beef, chicken, or veggies. And they're a steal at only $1.50 each, although it takes several to make a full meal. The rest of the menu is equally simple: baked jerk chicken, curry stews, seasoned rice with peas, and a handful of sides. But you may still have trouble deciding.

The most expensive menu item at Patties of Jamaica is oxtail stew. It costs $12 and is available only on Tuesdays and Thursdays.

Despite its obscure location, Patties of Jamaica has built a loyal customer base for its authentic and inexpensive Jamaican hand pies, stews, and jerk chicken dishes.

PATTIES OF JAMAICA

WHAT A well-kept Caribbean secret

WHERE 5172 Allisonville Rd.

COST $1.50 per patty

PRO TIP Patties of Jamaica sells frozen patties at $12 to $13 per dozen. Keep a bag or two at home for quick snacks and easy weeknight meals.

For more under-the-radar ethnic eats, try Mama's Korean Restaurant on Pendleton Pike or Kimu Restaurant in Greenwood. Kimu caters to a growing number of Chin refugees from Myanmar, as Indy now has the world's largest Chin population outside of Southeast Asia.

88

AN ODD ARTWORK AT THE ALEXANDER

Why is one woman's portrait made entirely of hair combs?

The Alexander is one of Indy's trendiest hotels, and it is best known for its artwork, from quirky sculptures to professionally executed graffiti. But the strangest work is a portrait of Hoosier legend Madam C. J. Walker. Created by artist Sonya Clark, it's made of 3,840 black combs—which makes sense if you know Walker's incredible story.

Walker was born in 1867 on the same Louisiana plantation where her parents had been slaves. Originally named Sarah Breedlove, she was orphaned at age seven, married at age fourteen, and widowed at age twenty with a daughter to support. She worked for many years as a laundress. When she developed a scalp disease and began losing her hair, she couldn't afford store-bought remedies. So she developed her own—and they worked. Hair products for African American women were rare then, so Walker had an untapped market for Madam C. J. Walker's Wonderful Hair Grower and eventually an entire hair-care product line. Walker became America's first self-made female millionaire, and she spread the wealth by opening beauty schools across the country to train stylists in her system, thus creating a path to prosperity for many other African American women.

Walker eventually moved her headquarters to Indianapolis, which had good transportation connections for shipping. One

---

In 1918, Walker built a mansion in Westchester County, New York, where her neighbors included the Rockefeller, Vanderbilt, and Tiffany families.

Born to former slaves in Louisiana, Madam C. J. Walker eventually became the nation's first self-made female millionaire. Photo courtesy Madam C. J. Walker Collection, Indiana Historical Society.

PORTRAIT OF MADAM C. J. WALKER

WHAT A fitting tribute to a self-made millionaire

WHERE The Alexander, 333 Delaware St., second-floor lounge

COST Free

PRO TIP Stop for a drink at the hotel's Plat 99 lounge; the beautiful glass pendant lights—ninety-nine in all—were designed by artist Jorge Pardo.

day, she visited a downtown theater and was told that ticket prices for African Americans had increased to twenty-five cents, while white people still had to pay only fifteen cents. So she simply built her own theater, creating a beloved gathering place for the African American community. Opened in 1927, the Madam Walker Legacy Center (617 Indiana Avenue) is now a National Historic Landmark. Currently closed for renovation, it will soon offer programming in the arts, financial literacy, leadership, entrepreneurship, and philanthropy.

89 THE MIDNIGHT TRAIN TO NOWHERE

Where in Indy can you still catch a sleeper train?

Landlocked Indianapolis owes much of its early economic prosperity to trains, which created new opportunities for travel and trade. That activity centered on Union Station, the first in the country to serve multiple independent railway companies under one roof. The existing building opened in 1888, and at its peak it welcomed two hundred passenger trains every day.

Starting in the 1970s, however, city leaders struggled to find a purpose for the historic building. Renovations in the 1980s, for example, transformed Union Station into a "festival marketplace" that was a notorious bust. But the project preserved the crumbling building and introduced an important new tenant: a thriving hotel.

The Crowne Plaza hotel chain now occupies the west portion of the station's former train shed, and it has found a unique way to preserve the building's heritage. Parked inside, still on their original tracks, are thirteen authentic 1920 Pullman cars that have been converted into twenty-six guest rooms. The Victorian ambiance is real, but it is conveniently offset by modern bathrooms and Wi-Fi. The hotel uses the station's former waiting room, a cathedral-like space with a soaring barrel-vaulted ceiling, as an event venue. And many of the station's architectural elements, such as steel arches and support girders, are still visible throughout the hotel.

Life-sized white "ghost" statues throughout the Crowne Plaza hotel depict the former denizens of Union Station, such as a train conductor, a newspaper boy, a porter, and various passengers.

The passenger waiting room at Union Station sits empty in this 1970 photo from the Historic American Buildings Survey. The beautiful space was neglected for many years, but it now serves as an event venue for the train-themed Crowne Plaza hotel. Photo courtesy the Library of Congress.

CROWNE PLAZA AT UNION STATION

WHAT Modern hotel rooms in converted Pullman train cars

WHERE Crowne Plaza, 123 W. Louisiana St.

COST $185 per night

NOTEWORTHY The Children's Museum of Indianapolis also houses an actual train: a fifty-five-ton Reuben Wells steam engine built in 1868.

90 AN ARTSY WAY TO STOP TRAFFIC

How did Indy transform its intersections into art galleries?

"When we see a blank surface, we paint it" might be a good way to describe Indy's recent approach to beautification. The city has dozens of new murals, and even underpass columns and manhole covers have gotten the artistic treatment. Throughout the city, meanwhile, more than fifty traffic signal control boxes have been transformed into "street-corner canvases" that celebrate each neighborhood's identity.

Irvington kicked off the trend in 2012, when seven control boxes were painted as part of the Great Indy Cleanup. That series, called "Bus Bike Walk Irvington," featured eco-friendly modes of transportation. The next year Irvington painted fourteen more control boxes, seven each in the "Car Culture" and "Farm Heritage" series.

Not to be outdone by Irvington, the Bates-Hendricks neighborhood soon covered its control boxes with gardens of

PAINTED TRAFFIC SIGNAL CONTROL BOXES

WHAT A city-wide series of "street-corner canvases"

WHERE Throughout the city

COST Free

PRO TIP Pressed for time? You'll find the densest concentrations of painted control boxes in the Irvington and Holy Cross neighborhoods.

The Arts Council of Indianapolis maintains a comprehensive directory of the city's public art, including nearly sixty painted traffic signal control boxes.

Graphic designer Andrea Light painted this stylized owl at the corner of East Washington Street and Emerson Avenue in 2017. The design, called Hoot, *won a contest sponsored by the Irvington Development Organization to paint the new box; the previous one had been destroyed in a car accident.*

irises. Control boxes in West Indianapolis now depict everything from flowers and arrows to racecars and an octopus. Those in Fishers are similarly varied, with images of an aquarium, a hot air balloon, musicians, daffodils, Canadian geese, and a train. And in the Holy Cross neighborhood, students from Arsenal Tech painted a dozen of the boxes along Michigan, New York, and Washington streets in 2016; one depicts the Indy skyline with a sky inspired by Vincent van Gogh's *Starry Night*. If you organize a scavenger hunt to track them all down, you'll find yourself exploring some of the city's most distinct and historic neighborhoods.

SOURCES

Antique Fan Collectors Association. "Antique Fan Museum." www.fanimation.com/museum.

Arts Council of Indianapolis. *Indy Arts Guide.* www.indyartsguide.org.

Baich, Laura, ed. *Undeniably Indiana: Hoosiers Tell the Story of Their Wacky and Wonderful State*. Bloomington, IN: Quarry Books, 2016.

Baker, Tom and Jonathan Tichenal. *Haunted Indianapolis and Other Indiana Ghost Stories*. Atglen, PA: Schiffer Publishing Ltd., 2008.

Bakken, Darrell J. *Now That Time Has Had Its Say: A History of the Indianapolis Central Canal, 1835–2002*. Bloomington, IN: Consolidated City of Indianapolis—Department of Waterworks, 2003.

Bakken, Dawn E. *On This Day in Indianapolis History*. Charleston, SC: The History Press, 2016.

Bennett, Amy. "Marian University's Connection to the Indianapolis Motor Speedway." Marian University (blog), February 13, 2017. www.marian.edu.

Blevins, Benjamin and Janneane Blevins, eds. *INDPLS Guide*. Indianapolis: PRINTtEXT, 2016.

Bodenhamer, David J. and Robert G. Barrows, eds. *The Encyclopedia of Indianapolis.* Bloomington, IN: Indiana University Press, 1994.

Boyce, Dianna. "John Wooden Sculpture Unveiled in Downtown Indianapolis." *Around Indy*, March 10, 2012.

British Museum. "The Parthenon Sculptures." www.britishmuseum.org/research/collection_online/collection_object_details.aspx?objectId=461666&partId=1&searchText=elgin+XLII&page=1.

Browne, Tiffany Benedict. "Friday Favorite: Circle Tower." Historic Indianapolis (blog), June 1, 2012. www.historicindianapolis.com/friday-favorite-circle-tower.

Browne, Tiffany Benedict. "Friday Favorite: Frieze Frame." Historic Indianapolis (blog), March 8, 2013. www.historicindianapolis.com/friday-favorite-frieze-frame.

Browne, Tiffany Benedict. "Indiana War Memorial, Shrine Room: Ten Elements Decoded." Historic Indianapolis (blog), April 7, 2012. www.historicindianapolis.com/indiana-war-memorial-shrine-room-10-elements-decoded.

Bundles, A'Lelia. *Madam Walker Theatre Center: An Indianapolis Treasure*. Charleston, SC: Arcadia Publishing, 2013.

Burrous, Ric. "Wooden in Bronze: First Public Art on Georgia Street Site." *IUPUI Magazine*, Spring 2012.

Butler University. "The Ballet Russe Scenery Collection of the Butler Ballet." www.butler.edu/dance/about/ballet-russe.

Butler University. "Dancing through Time: New Exhibit Highlights Butler's Tradition of Ballet Excellence." www.butler.edu/dance/about/dancingthroughtime.

Butler University. "Rare Books and Special Collections." www.butler.edu/library/collections/rare-special.

Caldwell, Howard. *The Golden Age of Indianapolis Theaters*. Bloomington, IN: Quarry Press, 2010.

Cathcart, Charlotte. *Indianapolis from Our Old Corner*. Indianapolis: Indiana Historical Society, 1965.

Cavinder, Fred D. *Forgotten Hoosiers: Profiles from Indiana's Hidden History*. Charleston, SC: The History Press, 2009.

Cavinder, Fred D. *More Amazing Tales from Indiana*. Bloomington, IN: Indiana University Press, 2003.

Citizens Energy Group. "DigIndy." www.citizensenergygroup.com/Our-Company/Our-Projects/Dig-Indy.

Connor, Lawrence S. *Star in the Hoosier Sky:* The Indianapolis Star *in the Years the City Came Alive, 1950–1990*. Carmel, IN: Hawthorne Publishing, 2006.

Cultural Landscape Foundation. "Butler University—Holcomb Gardens."
www.tclf.org/butler-university-holcomb-gardens.

Davis, Aleck. *Centennial History of Indiana: 1816–1916* (pamphlet in the collection of the Indiana Historical Society).

Disciples Home Missions. “Peace Pole.” www.discipleshomemissions.org/missions-advocacy/peace-pole.

Duffy, Reid. *Reid Duffy’s Guide to Indiana’s Favorite Restaurants*. Bloomington, IN: Quarry Books, 2006.

Dunn, Jacob Piatt. *Greater Indianapolis: The History, the Industries, the Institutions, and the People of a City of Homes, Volume 1*. Chicago: Lewis Publishing Company, 1910.

“Farming in the Sky.” Eskenazi Health (blog), May 10, 2016. www.eskenazihealth.edu/news/farming-in-the-sky.

Fernandez, Megan. “A Love Letter to the Idle.” *Indianapolis Monthly*, December 2018.

Fernandez, Megan. “This New Park Might Be the Most Unusual One in the Country.” *Indianapolis Monthly*, September 2018.

Finch, L. Mark. “Tuckaway: Imprinted by the Hands of Time.” *Indy Midtown Magazine*, October 27, 2017.

Fletcher, Calvin. *The Diary of Calvin Fletcher, Volume 1: 1817–1838.* Ed. Gayle Thornbrough. Indianapolis: Indiana Historical Society, 1972.

Forsyth, William. *Art in Indiana.* Indianapolis: The H. Lieber Company, 1916 (in the collection of the Indiana Historical Society).

Geib, George W. “The William F. Charters Collection: An Introduction.” Indianapolis: Butler University College of Liberal Arts and Sciences, 1994. www.digitalcommons.butler.edu/facsch_papers/801.

Gadski, Mary Ellen, ed. *Indianapolis Architecture: Transformations Since 1975*. Indianapolis: Indiana Architectural Foundation, 1993.

Goldberger, Paul. “Kevin Roche, Architect Who Melded Bold with Elegant, Dies at 96.” *New York Times*, March 2, 2019.

Gong, Dave. “Indy’s Sky Farm a Hint of Riverfront’s Future.” *Journal Gazette*, November 11, 2018.

Hamlett, Ryan. "The Devil in the Old Northside." Historic Indianapolis (blog), February 25, 2014. www.historicindianapolis.com/the-devil-in-the-old-northside-2.

Hamlett, Ryan. "The House of Blue Lights." Historic Indianapolis (blog), October 29, 2013. www.historicindianapolis.com/the-house-of-blue-lights.

Hamlett, Ryan. "Karl Bitter, Elmer Taflinger, and the Holliday Park Ruins." Historic Indianapolis (blog), May 20, 2014. www.historicindianapolis.com/karl-bitter-elmer-taflinger-and-the-holliday-park-ruins.

Hanlin, George R. *Remembering Indianapolis*. Nashville: Turner Publishing Company, 2010.

Harris, Bill. *Indianapolis: An Illustrated History.* San Marcos, CA: Heritage Media Corp., 2004.

Harry, Lou. "John Wooden Sculpture Awkwardly Earns National Attention." *Indianapolis Business Journal* (blog), November 20, 2012. www.ibj.com/blogs/1-lou-harry-s-a-e/post/38031-john-wooden-sculpture-awkwardly-earns-national-attention?v=preview.

Heal, Ron. "Koorsen Fire Museum." *Fire Apparatus & Emergency Equipment*, May 22, 2017.

Hicks, Patricia Brinkman. "Memories of Skiles Test and the House of Blue Lights." www.testfamilygenealogy.net/Documents/Quotes/Hickman.html.

Higgins, Will. "A Black Life that Mattered in Indy in 1836." *Indianapolis Star*, September 28, 2016.

Higgins, Will. "At His Death, 'Mr. Big' Left Gaudy Northside Indianapolis Home in Shambles." *Indianapolis Star*, December 9, 2013.

Higgins, Will. "During Vietnam 'the Army Wanted a Little Happy News': How Iconic Indianapolis Bakery Started." *Indianapolis Star*, December 17, 2018.

Higgins, Will. "Explore Indy's Rat-Infested Underworld." *Indianapolis Star*, October 31, 2013.

Higgins, Will. "True Story: Indy's Squirrel Invasion of 1822." *Indianapolis Star*, August 4, 2017.

Hindu Temple of Central Indiana. "Come on a Temple Tour." www.htci.org/visitor-info/tours.

Holy Rosary Catholic Church. "The Extraordinary Form at Holy Rosary." www.holyrosaryindy.org/latin.html.

Hunter, Alan E. and Russ Simnick. *Irvington Haunts: Haunted and Infamous Irvington*. Westfield, IN: Haunted History Publishing, 2004.

Hunter, Alan E. and Russ Simnick. *More Irvington Haunts.* Westfield, IN: Haunted History Publishing, 2008.

Huxtable, Ada Louise. "From Soaring Statements to Shoddy Mediocrity." *New York Times*, November 10, 1974.

Indiana Historical Bureau. "James Overall." www.in.gov/history/markers/4323.htm.

Indiana State Museum Foundation. *The Art of the 92 County Walk*. Indianapolis: Indiana State Museum Foundation, 2003.

Indiana State Museum: Stone, Steel, and Spirit. Cincinnati: Emmis Books, 2004.

Indianapolis 250,000: Souvenir of Indianapolis, 1907–1908, ed. The Commercial Club (pamphlet in the collection of the Indiana Historical Society).

Indianapolis Art Center. "ArtsPark." www.indplsartcenter.org/artspark.

Indianapolis Cultural Trail. "Chatham Passage by Sean Derry." www.indyculturaltrail.org/ictart/chatham-passage.

Indianapolis First Friends. "Our Community." www.indyfriends.org/what.

Indy Parks and Recreation. "Woolens Gardens Park." www.funfinder.indy.gov/#/details/78.

Jesse, Michael, ed. *Indianapolis Through Our Eyes:* The Indianapolis Star*, 1903–2003*. Battle Ground, WA: Pediment Publishing, 2003.

Johnson, Howard. *A Home in the Woods: Pioneer Life in Indiana*. Bloomington, IN: Indiana University Press, 1991.

Jones, C. S. and Henry T. Williams. *Ladies' Fancywork: Hints and Helps to Home Taste and Recreations*. New York: Henry T. Williams, 1876.

Kamm, Jeffrey S. *Classic Restaurants of Indianapolis*. Charleston, SC: American Palate, 2016.

Kennedy, Robert F. "Statement on Assassination of Martin Luther King Jr. in Indianapolis, Indiana, April 4, 1968." www.jfklibrary.org.

Lee, Ellen Wardell, Anne Robinson, and Alexandra Bonfante-Warren, eds. *Indianapolis Museum of Art: Highlights of the Collection*. Indianapolis: Indianapolis Museum of Art, 2005.

Lilly, Eli. *Prehistoric Antiquities of Indiana*. Indianapolis: Indiana Historical Society, 1937.

Lindquist, David. "Artist Clashes with 'Malicious' Recordface over Broad Ripple Mural." *Indianapolis Star*, October 24, 2017.

Lindquist, David. "The Mysterious Case of Recordface, the Street Art that Captivates and Irritates." *Indianapolis Star*, October 9, 2017.

Lorentz, Lisa. "Friday Favorite: Haunted Hannah House." Historic Indianapolis (blog), October 25, 2013. www.historicindianapolis.com/friday-favorites-haunted-hannah-house.

Lorentz, Lisa. "Friday Favorite: Hidden Gems." Historic Indianapolis (blog), November 1, 2013. www.historicindianapolis.com/friday-favorites-hidden-gems.

Lynch, Amy. "What in the World Is a Chicken Limo?" Visit Indiana (blog), May 18, 2018. www.visitindiana.com/blog/index.php/2018/05/18/indy-chicken-limo.

Mack, Justin L. "Thousands Celebrate Rebirth of Indy Hindu Temple." *Indianapolis Star*, June 7, 2015.

Mallett, Ann. *A Child's History of Indianapolis*. Indianapolis: Indianapolis Public Schools, 1966.

Maloney, Michael and Kenneth J. Remenschneider. *Indianapolis Landscape Architecture*. Washington, DC: Landscape Architecture Foundation, 1983.

Mannheimer, Steve. "A Big Brushoff." *Indianapolis Star*, July 29, 1997.

Marimen, Mark. *Haunted Indiana 3*. Holt, MI: Thunder Bay Press, 2001.

Marimen, Mark. *Haunted Indiana 4*. Holt, MI: Thunder Bay Press, 2005.

Marimen, Mark, James A. Willis, and Troy Taylor. *Weird Indiana: Your Travel Guide to Indiana's Local Legends and Best-Kept Secrets*. New York: Sterling, 2008.

Mitchell, Dawn. "Whatever Happened to Choc-Ola?" *Indianapolis Star*, July 18, 2016.

"Nature Study Club Formed." *Indianapolis Star*, January 4, 1908.

Neal, Andrea. *Road Trip: A Pocket History of Indiana*. Indianapolis: Indiana Historical Society Press, 2016.

Neal, Meg. "Pogue's Run." *Atlas Obscura*. www.atlasobscura.com/places/pogues-run.

Nye, Charlie, ed. *Hoosier Century: 100 Years of Photographs from* The Indianapolis Star *and* The Indianapolis News. United States: Sports Publishing Inc., 1999.

Olson, Scott. "Local Architectural Firm Woollen Molzan Disbands." *Indianapolis Business Journal*, April 27, 2011.

OneAmerica. "Time Flies When You're Having Pun." www.oneamerica.com/about-us/in-the-community/signboard.

Petry, Ashley. *100 Things to Do in Indianapolis Before You Die, Second Edition*. St. Louis: Reedy Press, 2018.

Pohlen, Jerome. *Oddball Indiana: A Guide to Some Really Strange Places*. Chicago: Chicago Review Press, 2002.

The Public Collection. "About." www.thepubliccollection.org/about.

The Public Collection. "Artists." www.thepubliccollection.org/artists.

Rose, Ernestine Bradford. *The Circle: The Center of Our Universe*. Indianapolis: Indiana Historical Society Publications, 1957.

Sankowsky, Lorri and Keri Young. *Ghost Hunter's Guide to Indianapolis*. Gretna, LA: Pelican Publishing Company, 2008.

Schmidt, Steven J. *The Architectural Treasures of the Indiana State Library*. Indianapolis: Indiana State Library, 2014.

Sharp, Wayne. *Legends in Blue: Selected Stories from the History of the Indianapolis Police Department, 1845–1965*. Westfield, IN: Hawthorne Publishing, 2002.

Sicotte, Jon. "The Growth Engine: Sun King Brewing Challenges State Laws to Grow Across Indiana Borders." *Brewer Magazine*, December 22, 2017.

Stall, Sam. "The Hoosierist: Angie's Dish." *Indianapolis Monthly*, June 2015.

Stall, Sam. "The Hoosierist: Bugging Out." *Indianapolis Monthly*, June 2012.

Stall, Sam. "The Hoosierist: Butt of the Joke." *Indianapolis Monthly*, December 2012.

Stall, Sam. "The Hoosierist: Criminal Rinds." *Indianapolis Monthly*, July 2015.

Stall, Sam. "How Indy Are You? Take the Quiz!" *Indianapolis Monthly*, June 2014.

Stall, Sam. "Who Killed Union Station?" *Indianapolis Monthly*, March 2016.

Stickney, Ida Stearns. *Civic Studies of Indianapolis: Number 1—Pioneer Indianapolis*. Indianapolis: The Bobbs-Merrill Company, 1907.

Stoner, Andrew E. *Wicked Indianapolis*. Charleston, SC: The History Press, 2011.

"Stop and Smell the Flowers." *The Butler Collegian*, September 27, 2011.

Sunkel, Gwen. "In the Park: Woollens Garden." Historic Indianapolis (blog), November 1, 2014. www.historicindianapolis.com/in-the-park-woollens-gardens.

Sutton, Susan. *Indianapolis: The Bass Photo Company Collection.* Indianapolis: Indiana Historical Society Press, 2008.

Tenuth, Jeffrey. *Indianapolis: A Circle City History.* Charleston, SC: Arcadia Publishing, 2004.

Veal's Ice Tree. www.vealsicetree.wixsite.com/vealsicetree.

Wang, Stephanie. "$10 Million Expansion of Indy Hindu Temple to Open in June." *Indianapolis Star*, March 18, 2015.

Werner, Nick. *Best Hikes Near Indianapolis*. Guilford, CT: Morris Book Publishing, 2012.

West, Evan. "Remember the Tigers: Crispus Attucks, 1955 State Basketball Champs." *Indianapolis Monthly*, March 2005.

Whitson, Jennifer. "Otterness Sculptures on Their Way Back to Indianapolis." *Indianapolis Business Journal*, May 21, 2007.

Willis, Wanda Lou. *Haunted Hoosier Trails*. Cincinnati: Clerisy Press, 2002.

Willis, Wanda Lou. *More Haunted Hoosier Trails.* Covington, KY: Clerisy Press, 2004.

Wilson-Rich, Noah. "Bees in the Big City." *Tufts Now*, November 23, 2015.

Winslow, Hattie Lou and Joseph R. H. Moore. *Camp Morton 1861–1865: Indianapolis Prison Camp*. Indianapolis: Indiana Historical Society, 1995.

Wittmeyer, Sara. "Indiana Plaque Marks a Presidential Tumble." *Weekend Edition Sunday*, National Public Radio, July 17, 2011.

Wolfsie, Dick. *Indiana Curiosities: Quirky Characters, Roadside Oddities, and Other Offbeat Stuff*. Guilford, CT: Morris Book Publishing, 2010.

Wyland Foundation. "Wyland Walls." www.wylandfoundation.org/community.php?subsection=wyland_walls.

Yost, Mark. "Taking Aim at an Old Debate." *Wall Street Journal*, February 23, 2012.

INDEX

3 Floyds Brewing, 44
46 for XLVI, 52–53
6Cents, 36
92 County Walk, 74–75
A Home in the Woods, 116
Acton, 86, 134–135
Alabaster Betty, 77
Alexander, The, 194–195
Allison Mansion, 154–155
Allison, James, 154–155
American United Life, 108
Ann Dancing, 16
Antique Fan Collectors Association, 130
Antique Fan Museum, 130–131
Arsenal Tech, 182–183, 199
Art Deco, 82–83
Art Dish, 146
Arts Council of Indianapolis, 52–53, 142, 198
ArtsPark, 80–81
Bad Axe Throwing, 118–119, 168
Bakery, 44, 176–177
Ballet Russe de Monte Carlo, The, 114–115
Barton Tower, 164
Basile History Market, 171
Bates-Hendricks neighborhood, 198
Battista, Tom, 39
Beekeepers of Indiana, The, 138–139
Big Car Collaborative, 160
Biltwell Event Center, 147
Birch Bayh Federal Building, 164
Bitter, Karl, 172
Black Friday, 44–45
Blass, Bill, 134
Bliss, Pamela, 52
Bluebeard, 39
Bobbs-Merrill Publishing Company, 33
Bocce, 168–169
Boy and Dog, 143
Bracken, Todd, 150–151
Bradbury, Keith, 12
Breakfast Magpie, 44–45
Brickhead 3, 16
Broad Ripple Art Fair, 81
Burkhart, David, 124
Burlesque Bingo Bango Show, 76–77
Bush Stadium, 38
Butler Ballet, 114
Butler University, 114–115, 144–145, 174–175
Buzzard's Roost, 2
Caldwell, Howard, 178
Camp Morton, 141
Canal Towpath, 145
Canal Walk, 53, 68
Cannon, Ruth, 19
Care/Don't Care, 16
Carmel Arts and Design District, 156
Carmichael, Mike and Glenda, 22
Central Canal, 171
Central State Hospital, 120
Chain Gang, 124
Chanel, Coco, 134
Charters, William F., 174–175
Chatham Passage, 16–17
Chicken Limo, 110–111
Children's Museum of Indianapolis, The, 59, 62–63, 184, 197
Choc-Ola, 8–9, 58
Christ Church Cathedral, 165
Circle City Athletics, 168

Circle City Curling Club, 20–21
Circle City Industrial Complex, 146–147
Circle Tower, 82–83
Citizens Energy Group, 122
City Gallery, 57
City Market, 83, 165, 190
City-County Building, 1, 136–137
Civil War, 69, 140–141, 182–183
Clark, Sonya, 194
Clinton, Bill, 113
Clowes Memorial Hall, 165
Coca-Cola bottling plant, 82
Cohron's Manufactured Homes, 58–59
College Life Insurance Company, 66–67
Colonel Eli Lilly Civil War Museum, 69
Colonel's Cupboard, 182–183
Color Fuses, 164
Columbia Club, 83
Community Unity, 162
Congregation Beth-El Zedeck, 48
Congressional Medal of Honor Memorial, 68
Conner Prairie, 171
Coprolites, 62–63
Crane Bay, 147
Crawford, Joan, 18
Crescendo, 81
Cricket, 168
Crispus Attucks High School, 182
Crow, Julie, 30
Crown Hill Cemetery, 27, 42–43, 79, 167
Crowne Plaza, 196–197
Cultural Landscape Foundation, The, 144
Cummins, 66
Curling lessons, 21
Dallara IndyCar Factory, 154
Dance Sophisticates, 36
Danilova, Alexandra, 114
Dark Lord Day, 44
Dauntless Sailing School, 150–151
Dean, James, 8, 74
Derry, Sean, 16
Detour, 36
Devil in the White City, 50
Devious, 36–37
Dick the Bruiser, 160
DigIndy Art Project, 122–123
DigIndy Tunnel System, 122
Dillinger, John, 43, 60–61
Dinosphere, 63
Dior, Christian, 134
Disney, Walt, 18–19
Doctor Who, 12–13
Donovan, Tara, 134
Doppler radar, 148
Dose, 36, 108–109
Doyle, Sir Arthur Conan, 157
Dracorex hogwartsia, 62
Drunkometer, 60
Duckpin bowling, 179
Duncan, Isadora, 18
Dunn, Jacob Piatt, 124
Eagle Creek Park, 59
Earhart, Amelia, 18, 62
Einstein, Albert, 18–19
Eiteljorg Museum of American Indians and Western Art, 142, 185
Elgin Marbles, 56
Emmerich Manual High School, 182
Eskenazi Health, 14–15, 191
Evening with the Authors, An, 76
Everhart, Joe, 19
FAB Crew, 36–37
Fall Creek Parkway Trail, 2–3
Female Tourist, 142–143

Festival of Ice, 87
First Fridays, 161
Fisher, Carl, 154–155
Fishers, Indiana, 171, 188, 199
Fletcher Place, 38
Fletcher, Calvin, 116–117, 124
Flowing Well Park, 172
Ford assembly plant, 147
Fossils, 62
Foucault pendulum, 46
Fountain Square, 36–38, 44–45, 76, 146, 160, 178–179
Fountain Square Theatre, 178–179
Frampton, Tom, 130
Free Money, 142–143
Freeman, John, 125
Frenchie, 36
Friends Meditational Woods, 48–49
Galyan's bear sculpture, 59
Garfield comic strip, 74
Garfield Park, 146, 160–161, 176
Garfield Park Conservatory, 176
Geist Lake Marina, 151
Geist Reservoir, 150–151
Gen Con, 152–153
Gershwin, George, 18–19
Glaser, Milton, 164–165
Gnomes, vi, 176–177
Goose the Market, 54
Graffiti, 10, 36–37, 194
Granada Theatre, 178
Graves, Michael, 80–81
Gravity Hill, 128–129
Gray Brothers Cafeteria, 129
Great Flood of 1913, 148
Great Indy Cleanup, 198
Great Squirrel Invasion of 1822, 116–117
Greater Indianapolis Progress Committee, 24
Green, John, 11
Guinness World Record, 22–23
Guyana, 162
Habig Garden Shop, 59
Halston, 134
Hannah House, 78–79
Hannah, Alexander, 78–79
Harmon, Tim, 30–31
Harrison Center for the Arts, 53, 57, 146
Harroun, Ray, 155
Harry, Lou, 70
Hawkins, Sir John, 174
Hawthorne Community Center, 190
Heidelberg Haus, 176–177
Herron High School, 56–57
Herron School of Art and Design, 57, 191
Herron-Morton Place, 140
Hindu Temple of Central Indiana, 72–73
Hippo Party Bus, 111
Historic Indianapolis, 2, 26
Holcomb Gardens, 144–145
Holcomb Memorial Carillon Tower, 144
Holcomb Observatory and Planetarium, 144
Holcomb, James, 144–145
Hollering, Christina, 123
Holliday Park, 1, 172–173
Holmes, H. H., 50
Holmes, Sherlock, 156
Holy Cross, 198–199
Holy Rosary Catholic Church, 126–127
Hoosier Hospitality on the Boatload of Knowledge, 52–53
Hoosier Poet, The, 166–167
Hoot, 199
Hostetler, Jerry Alan, 180–181
House of Blue Lights, The, 26–27

Hsu, Louis and Nancy, 132
Hudnall, Katie, 191
Huff, Doug, 35
Huxtable, Ada Louise, 136
Hyde, Esther Hall, 47
Iaria, Dan, 9
Ichiban Noodles, 132–133
Ichiban Sushi Bar, 133
Idle: A Point of View, The, 38–39
Imperial Breakfast Magpie, 44–45
Indiana Basketball Hall of Fame, 59
Indiana Bee School, 138–139
Indiana Comic Con, 152
Indiana Convention Center, 142–143
Indiana Ghost Tours, 51
Indiana High School Athletic Association, 182
Indiana Historical Bureau, 32, 125
Indiana Historical Society, 19, 85, 141, 163–165, 170–171, 179, 195
Indiana History Center, 85, 170–171
Indiana Landmarks, 34, 83, 125
Indiana Medical History Museum, 120–121
Indiana Nature Study Club, 2
Indiana Repertory Theatre, 165
Indiana State Fair, 28–29, 139
Indiana State Library, 32–33
Indiana State Museum, 1, 46–47, 74–75, 185
Indiana State Police Museum, 60–61
Indiana State University, 71
Indiana War Memorial, 1, 68–69
Indiana War Memorial Museum, 69
Indianapolis Art League, 80
Indianapolis Business Journal, 70
Indianapolis Cultural Trail, 17, 38–39, 122–123
Indianapolis Fencing Club, 168
Indianapolis First Friends, 48–49
Indianapolis Greenway Canal, 144
Indianapolis High School, 182
Indianapolis Monthly, 24, 38, 70, 110
Indianapolis Motor Speedway Museum, 154
Indianapolis Museum of Art, 134–135, 160
Indianapolis Public Library, 190
Indianapolis Public Schools, 183
Indianapolis Scottish Highland Games, 168–169
Indianapolis Star, The, 2, 4, 36, 168
Indianapolis Super Bowl Host Committee, 70
Indianapolis Water Company, 122
Indianapolis World Sports Park, 168
Indianapolis Zoo, 142, 185
Indy 500, 1, 154–155
Indy Arts Guide, 16
Indy Cycloplex, 168–169
Indy Story Slam, 84–85
Indy Synchro, 168–169
IndyFringe Basile Theatre, 84
Infamous with Style, 36
International Harvester, 8
Irvington, 9, 50–51, 198–199
Irwin Library, 175
Italian Street Festival, 126
IUPUI, 57, 123, 169
James Whitcomb Riley Boyhood Home and Museum, 167
James Whitcomb Riley Museum Home, 166–167
John Morton-Finney Center for Educational Services, 24
John's Famous Stew, 158–159
Johnson, Oliver, 51, 116
Jones, Jim, 162–163

Jonestown, 162
Jordan, David Starr, 174
Jungbauer, Juergen, 176–177
Just Pop In, 54
Karinska, Barbara, 114
Keene, Ken, 19
Kennedy, Robert F., 112–113
Kennedy, Ted, 112–113
Kennedy-King National Commemorative Site, 112–113
Kimu Restaurant, 193
King, Martin Luther, Jr., 62, 82, 112–113, 188–189
Kinney, Belle, 140
Koorsen Fire and Security, 6–7
Koorsen Fire Museum, 6–7, 60
Koorsen, Randy, 6–7
Ku Klux Klan, 1, 50–51, 182
Landmark for Peace, 113
Leach, David, 124–125
Lennon, John, 39
Let's Make a Date Gameshow, 76
Light, Andrea, 199
Lilly Oncology on Canvas, 36
Lilly, Eli, 64, 69
Lincoln, Abraham, 47, 74
Lindberg, Arthur, 144
Lindquist, David, 4
Linear bocce, 168–169
Lions' Paws: The Story of Famous Hands, 18
Little Orphant Annie, 166
Llama costume contest, 28
Lloyd and Harvey's Wowie Zowie Show, 76
Lockerbie, 167
Lombard, Carole, 18
Long's Bakery, 44
Love Letter Indiana, 53
Lucas Oil Stadium, 137
Madam C. J. Walker's Wonderful Hair Grower, 194
Madam Walker Legacy Center, 195
Majestic Building, 165
Male Tourist, 142–143
Mama's Korean Restaurant, 193
Manhole covers, 122–123, 198
Manson, Charles, 163
Marian University, 154–155
Marmon Motor Company, 155
Marmon Wasp, 155
Martinsville High School, 71
Massachusetts Avenue Cultural District, 16
McCutcheon, Brian, 190
McNaughton, John, 80
McQuiston, James, 24–25
Mead, 44–45, 138
Meier, George, 18–19
Meier, Nellie, 18–19
Mellencamp, John, 28
Meridian Park, 18
Metro Nightclub, 17
Mile Square, 10, 74
Miller, J. Irwin, 66
Millionaires Row, 154–155
Minton-Capehart Federal Building, 164–165
Mist, 29
Monroe, Marilyn, 8
Monument Circle, 82–83, 137, 190
Moon tree, 107
Morning Magnolias, 53
Morphos, 53
Morton, Oliver, 140
Mr. Bendo, 58–59
Mr. Big, 180–181
Mug-n-Bun, 40
Muncie, Dorgan, 77
Muncie, Milroy, 77
Munds, Ellen, 84
Mural, 24–25, 36, 52–53, 81, 147, 160, 164–165

Museum of Miniature Houses and Other Collections, The, 156–157
My Affair with Kurt Vonnegut, 52
National Collegiate Athletic Association, 184
National Register of Historic Places, 19
National Road, 34, 106
National Weather Service Forecast Office, 148–149
Nautilus, 191
Navistar, 8
NCAA Hall of Champions, 184–185
New Day Craft, 36–37, 44–45, 77
New Harmony, Indiana, 52
NOAA Weather Radio, 148
Normington, Harry, Sr., 8
Nutcracker, The, 114
O'Brien, Frederick, 174
Oasis Diner, 34–35
Oberholtzer, Madge, 50–51
Old Pathology Building, 120
Oliver Phase, 64–65
On the Banks of Plum Creek, 116
OneAmerica, 108–109
Opie, Julian, 16
Orcas Passage, 24–25
Otterness, Tom, 142–143
Our Lady of the Most Holy Rosary, 126–127
Overall, James, 124–125
Owen, Richard, 140–141
Owen, Robert, 52
Pace, Merle, 123
Pardo, Jorge, 195
Park of the Laments, 38
Parthenon, 56–57
Partington, Brose, 190
Pathways to Peace Garden, 49
Patties of Jamaica, 192–193
Pawlus, Jamie, 16
Peace Pole, 48–49
People for Urban Progress, 38
Peppy Grill, 8
Percussive Arts Society, 186
Persephone, 144–145
Pickleball, 168–169
Plat 99, 195
Plump, Bobby, 47
Pogue, George, 10–11
Pogue's Run, 10–11
Prehistoric Antiquities of Indiana, 64
Prest-O-Lite Company, 154
Public Collection, 190–191
Pullman cars, 196
Purdue University, 71
Pyle, Ernie, 47
Pyramids, The, 66–67
Quetzalcoatl Returns to Look in the Mirror, 53
Races of Man, The, 172–173
Rachmaninoff, Sergei, 18–19
Raggedy Ann, 166
Raggedy Man, The, 166
Ragsdale, Kyle, 52–53
Ralph's Muffler & Brake Service, 58
Ralston, Alexander, 10
Ramsay, Ken, 19
Rapp, George, 52
Rathskeller, The, 158
Real Silk Hosiery Mill, 16
Recordface, 4–5
Rector, Don, 35
Redenbacher, Orville, 28
Religious Society of Friends, 48
Restoration Baptist Church, 163
Return to Innocence, 53
Reuben Wells steam engine, 197
Rhythm! Discovery Center, 186–187
Riley Children's Foundation, 166
Riley Hospital for Children, 166
Riley, James Whitcomb, 166–167

Ripley, William, 62
Rivoli Park Labyrinth, 48
Roche, Kevin, 66–67
Rock-Cola 1950s Café, 8–9
Rocket Doll Revue, 76
Roosevelt, Eleanor, 18–19
Roosevelt, Franklin, 18–19
Rubush and Hunter, 82
Ruins, The, 1, 172–173
Runners, The, 24
Russell Hall, 57
Ryan, Leo J., 162
Saarinen, Eero, 66–67
Sacred317, 36
Schmidt, Steven J., 32
Schrott Center for the Arts, 114–115
Schwitzer Corporation, 146
Scottish Rite, 164
Second Vatican Council, 126
Seung, Henry and Theresa, 192
Shapiro's Delicatessen, 158
Sharp, Wayne, 42
*Shortridge Daily Ech*o, 182
Shortridge High School, 182
Shrine Room, 68
Simon, Rachel M., 191
Six Points, 34
Skiles Test Nature Park, 2, 27
Sky Farm, 14–15
Slippery Noodle, 78, 158
Smoking Goose Meat School, 54–55
Smoking Goose Meatery, 54–55
Snepp, Amanda Snyder, 47
Soldiers and Sailors Monument, 69, 82
Sometimes I Sits, 80
Speedbeard, 36
Sports Legends Experience, 184
St. Elmo Steak House, 158
St. Paul Building, 172
Stall, Sam, 70
Stardust Terrace Café, 171
Statehouse, 107, 137, 141, 143
Statue of Liberty, 30–31
Stephenson, D. C., 50–51
Stokely-Wheeler Mansion, 155
Storytelling Arts of Indiana, 84–85
Strangeff, Dapa, 158
Strangeff, Mike, 158
Strangeff, Steve, 158
Stratton-Porter, Gene, 166
Strawtown Koteewi Park, 64–65
Stutz Artists Open House, 147
Stutz Business and Arts Center, 146
Stutz Motorcar Company, 146
Subsurface Graffiti Expo, 36–37
Sugar-cream pie, 8
Suh, Do-Ho, 134
Sun King Brewery, 188–189
Super Bowl, 53, 70
Swing dances, 178–179
Table Tennis Club of Indianapolis, 168
Tallchief, Maria, 114
Tarkington, Booth, 166, 182
Taylor Center of Natural History, 64–65
Taylor, Marshall "Major," 64–65, 169
Teeny Statue of Liberty Museum, 30–31
Test, Skiles, 2, 26–27
Thomas E. Willey Memorial Rock Garden, 145
Throop, Pam, 157
Tibbs Drive-In Theatre, 40–41
Tim and Julie's Another Fine Mess, 30
Tolbert, Mpozi Mshale, 36
Tom Otterness in Indianapolis, 142–143

Torluemke, Tom, 190
Toussaint, Armand, 144
Tower Realty Company, 82
Traffic signal control boxes, 198
Tridentine Mass, 126–127
Tube Factory Artspace, 146–147, 160–161
Tuckaway, 18–19
Turrell, James, 134–135
Turtles All the Way Down, 11
Twice Under, 11
Twisted House, 80–81
Underground Airlines, 11
Underground Railroad, 78–79, 124
Union Station, 165, 196–197
Upland Free Time Movie Series, 76
Urban homesteading, 138
US Weather Bureau, 148
USS *Indianapolis*, 68
Van Buren Elm, 106
Van Buren, Martin, 106–107
Veal, Vierl G., 86–87
Veal's Ice Tree, 86
Verdak, George, 114–115
Victory Field, 185
Vonnegut, Kurt, 52, 182
Wakefield, Dan, 182
Walk of Legends, 28
Walker, Madam C. J., 194–195
Waterflow, 53
Western Electric Company, 172
Wheeler, Frank, 154–155
Whipple, Mindy, 123
White Rabbit Cabaret, 76–77
White River Canal Aquaculture Preservation Aquarium, 53
White River State Park, 68, 74, 152, 185
White, Ella, 29
Whitfield, William, 42–43
Who North America, 12–13
Wilder, Laura Ingalls, 116
Williams, G. Monty, 154–155
Williams, J. Scott, 32
Willy Wonka and the Chocolate Factory, 62
Winterlights, 135
Winters, Ben H., 11
Wooden, John, 70–71
Wooden's Legacy, 70–71
Woollen Associates, 164
Woollen, Molzan & Partners, 164
Woollen, William Watson, 2–3
Woollen's Garden of Birds and Botany, 2–3
Workingman's Friend, 158
Works Progress Administration, 80
World Axe Throwing League, 118
World's Largest Ball of Paint, The, 22–23
Wyland, Robert, 24–25
Young Beekeeper Program, 139
Zesco Restaurant Supply, 59
Zionsville, Indiana, 130–131